Life Is Friends

A COMPLETE GUIDE TO THE LOST ART
OF CONNECTING IN PERSON

Jeanne Martinet

Stewart, Tabori & Chang
New York

Published in 2009 by Stewart, Tabori & Chang
An imprint of Harry N. Abrams, Inc.

Library of Congress Cataloging-in-Publication Data

Martinet, Jeanne
 Life is friends : a complete guide to the lost art of connecting in person
/ Jeanne Martinet.
   p. cm.
1. Friendship. 2. Hospitality. I. Title.
BJ1533.F8M32 2009
158.2'5--dc22
                        2008043284

Editor: Jennifer Levesque
Designer: LeAnna Weller Smith
Production Manager: Tina Cameron
Indexer: Nancy Wolff

The text of this book was composed in Corporate S and Filosophia.

Printed and bound in the United States
10 9 8 7 6 5 4 3 2 1

HNA
harry n. abrams, inc.
a subsidiary of La Martinière Groupe
115 West 18th Street
New York, NY 10011
www.hnabooks.com

Contents

ACKNOWLEDGMENTS

I would like to thank my very savvy editor, Jennifer Levesque, along with everyone else at Stewart, Tabori, and Chang, for their enthusiasm and support. My agent, Liza Dawson, is the best agent a writer could have, and I am enormously grateful to her. But most of all, I need to thank my friends—some of whom were integral to the writing of this book, but all of whom are integral to my life.

Disclaimer: Names and places in this book have been changed to protect my social life.

Who Killed the Dinner Party?

I n addition to food, shelter, and sex, humans need companionship. We crave friendship as much as we crave heat when we are cold or water when we are thirsty. But do we really know how to go about getting it?

Not too long ago, I attended a friend's birthday party, held at a chic bar in Tribeca. It was a typical Manhattan venue: 1950s Palm Springs decor, dim lighting, loud techno-fusion music, and seemingly impenetrable clusters of people around the bar and the buffet table. Being an intrepid mingler, I was not daunted. I dove in.

After ten minutes or so, I spotted a tall man by himself off to one side of the buffet table. He was quite handsome, but what really made him interesting to me was that he was not maneuvering to get to the food but seemed more interested in scoping out the people. *How evolved*, I thought. I approached him and introduced myself. To my delight, I learned that he was someone I had once spoken to on the phone—a freelance editor named Karl, who lived in my very own Manhattan neighborhood. He had definite friend potential. I could already imagine us meeting for coffee.

When I mentioned I was the author of *The Art of Mingling,* Karl immediately asked me if I had written any books on Internet mingling. My reply to him was what it always is when people ask me this: that as far as I am concerned, there is no such thing as mingling on the Internet, and that all true forms of socializing are practiced face-to-face. Somewhat taken aback, Karl insisted that the Internet was a "great place to mingle." He told me that he had many online friends with whom he kept in constant contact; he was active in several sports chat rooms and contributed regularly to various blogs—his own and others. He received and wrote dozens of e-mails a day.

"Well," I said, trying to choose my words carefully, "do you regularly see these cyber-friends? In the outside world?" I can't help it, I am always interviewing people about their social lives.

"Not really. Most of them live in other cities." He paused, looking a tad embarrassed. "And by the time I get through work, the gym, and catching up on my e-mail . . . " He caught my eye and we both laughed. "Okay, you got me. I guess I don't go out very much."

Karl, like many people, was a fairly serious webhead. Yet I could tell he was someone who had a real desire to connect with people. It was obvious he *liked* people. He was an engaging conversationalist; he certainly wasn't an introvert. So what was stopping Karl from being able to transfer his social energy from his virtual life to his real life?

Most people are open to meeting new people and eager to make friends. Indeed, the pervasiveness of the Internet in our lives—and the staggering popularity of sites like Match.com, Facebook, and MySpace—shows just how much we hunger for connection. The Internet provides the ultimate pathway to other people. However, the miracle of being able to e-mail (or video chat with) people anywhere in the world often blinds us to the fact that this technology is a means to an end, not the end itself. We now have instant access to an unlimited number of people, but how do we go from sharing our profile with someone to becoming good friends? Many teens brag about having hundreds of "friends" on Facebook, but how many of these are real friendships? An acquaintance told me her daughter has a relationship with a boy that has been going on for months which is almost exclusively an electronic one—texting, IMing, and cell phone calls. The daughter believes she and this boy are very much in love, but her mother can't help wondering what their relationship would be like if they were spending actual time together.

Ironically, as we become more and more involved with communication technology, we seem to be communicating less and less. Out on the street, in the elevator, in the coffee shop, in the checkout line at the store—practically everyone has a Bluetooth device in their ear and is talking to someone, but hardly ever to the person right in front of them. When you Google "socializing," you find all kinds of sites that deal with how to cyber-network, but very few on the art of the perfect dinner party. Nevertheless, all of us desire social intimacy, as people have since the beginning of time.

"Don't feel bad," I said to Karl, "Going out to meet new people can be hard. But what about hanging out with friends you already have? For instance, when is the last time you had a friend over to dinner?"

He squinted off into space for a moment. Then he looked sheepish, and also a little surprised. "Um...2004?"

A little while later, I left Karl to find Susie, our super-gregarious hostess and the birthday girl. I spotted her over in the far corner, waving hello at someone with one hand and holding her cell phone

to her ear with the other. Because of her job in PR, Susie went out
five nights a week, attended all the trendy openings, and seemed
to know everyone in New York City. She laughed when I told her
I had met Karl and that I was trying to wean him away from his
computer. She said that even though she had been working with
him for more than a year, this was the very first time she had seen
him in the flesh.

"The first and—who knows—maybe the last time," she said.
"Since actually I'm thinking of moving."

Surprised, I asked Susie where she was going. I assumed it
was to some fabulous job in L.A., or maybe Paris.

"I'm not sure. But I'm sick of it here. I just can't seem to make
any friends." She looked wistful. My head was spinning. Susie?
Socialite Susie? *No friends*?

"What are you talking about? You know more people than
Oprah!"

She shook her head. "No, I mean, I don't have any close
friends. I don't have any *best* friends. Even when I was with David,
we just saw only each other all weekend."

"But...all those parties, I'm always so envious..."

"Oh, I know it sounds wonderful," said Susie. "And yes, it's
fun, but, well, I don't feel...connected. It doesn't feel meaningful.
I feel something is missing."

Though I was shocked to hear this kind of thing from Susie, I
was not unfamiliar with the complaint. I have been writing and
talking about social mores for fifteen years, and I am quite used
to people telling me how frustrated they are with trying to socialize at large gatherings. In fact, one of the main reasons people
give for not wanting to put themselves into mingling situations
is that they don't see the point of it. Many have said to me, "Why

should I bother trying to talk to a bunch of strangers who I'll never see again?" What I have realized after hearing this so often is that what they really mean is that they don't know how to go from meeting a person to building a real friendship with that person.

While Karl was living a virtual social life, Susie was living a sound-bite social life. The pressures of the twenty-first century encourage us to skate along the surface of things, and to do as much as we can as quickly as possible. Everything is deliverable and disposable, and quantity has replaced quality to such a large extent that it no longer seems like a bad tradeoff.

"What about dinner parties?" I asked Susie, musing aloud. "Do you at least have a few people you see regularly for relaxed dinners?"

"Not really. I'm too busy to give dinners, and besides I can't really cook. Everyone I know goes out to restaurants."

I smiled knowingly. "And there are usually fifteen people there and you spend most of the evening trying to figure out what the people at the far end of the table are laughing about?"

"Exactly," Susie sighed.

"So when is the last time you had someone over to your place?"

"I threw a cocktail party last year.... No wait, that was the year before. So I guess, two years ago." She looked at me as if I were about to give her a medical diagnosis. "Is that bad?"

I laughed and squeezed her arm reassuringly. "No, not at all!" God, first I practically grilled Karl and now I was spooking the hostess. "It's just that I have this theory that socializing at home is somehow the key."

When I was seven, a girl named Beth moved into our neighborhood. Within one week, Beth had been to my house to play (or I had been to hers) at least six times. We already had "inside jokes" that would send us into fits of giggles. We knew everything that was in each other's closets; I knew that her favorite Troll was the one with red hair she had braided so tightly she couldn't get it undone, and she knew that my collection of plastic Rat Finks included two I had swiped from my older brother. We had to add an extra hour onto each of our playdates because first she would walk me home, and then I would walk her home, and then she would walk me home again. I think we would do this until it got dark, or until a parent came to get us.

Children tend to develop intimate relationships very quickly. One of the main reasons for this is that almost immediately upon making friends, children go over to play at each other's houses. When you have someone over, you are, in a sense, revealing yourself. You are sharing who you are and how you live. For adults as well as children, socializing with friends at your or at their house is how you foster closeness; it is the most important part of the lifelong conversation that is involved in friendship-building. After all, where does the term "housewarming" come from? Do you turn the heat up for a housewarming? No. Having friends in your house "warms" it—puts love in it. It's as if it's not really ready to be your home until you have people over.

I have noticed lately that even extremely social people seem unwilling to make a regular habit of inviting people to their homes. They say it's too much trouble. They say they don't have time, that their apartment is a mess, that they don't know what to serve, or that they are afraid guests won't get along (or that if they put their friends together in an intimate setting, they will start talking about their host!). It's a lot easier just to go out. Why try to get up a dinner party for your birthday when there are so many restaurants and it takes so little effort to make the reservation and send an eVite to everyone? While those who live in the suburbs tend to have people over more than those who live in cities, they still complain to me that their social life is not satisfying, that they always have dinner with the same neighbors from across the street and don't really get anything out of it, or that everyone ends up watching the football game during dinner. A lot of couples who have kids are often too busy micro-managing the children all weekend to think about entertaining. Mostly, people—no matter where they live—confess to me that they feel they don't cook well enough. The general consensus seems to be that the fare must be gourmet or you can't have people over.

What I want to know is: When did we all start having to be Emeril? Didn't our parents invite people over for cold cuts and potato salad? Mine did. (Of course, it may have been easier with my mother at home doing the cooking, but it's still doable). In any case, having people over doesn't necessitate your giving a conventional dinner party; you can ask someone over for coffee and croissants, or have a group over for drinks or a casual card game. The important thing is that you are opening your home to friends. When my parents were courting, their dates consisted of going to their best friends' house for ice cream and conversation. In fact, I might not even exist if my parents' newlywed friends hadn't been willing to say, "Come on over!" No one worried that much about whether or not the hosts had vacuumed or what kind of ice cream they were eating. They knew that it wasn't about the food, the ambiance, or impressing anyone. It was about fun and friendship. And friendship is as important as marriage, kids, or money.

In times past, the idea of a week going by without a dinner with friends or a house party was unthinkable. The (albeit fictional) Bennets in *Pride and Prejudice* dined with "four and twenty families," and when Mrs. Bennet wanted her daughter Jane to catch a husband, she made sure she was forced (by inclement weather and lack of a carriage) to stay over at the gentleman's house. Why? Because being in someone's home helps to cultivate intimacy with that person.

It's also a fact that when encountering new people—friends of a friend, for example—it tends to socially "stick" better if you socialize with them at the mutual friend's house. When I meet someone at a restaurant or some other public venue, I seldom see them again; but if I meet them at a friend's house, where we are more relaxed and where the hospitality of the host acts as a fertile ground for budding friendships, it often develops into a new relationship. Obviously you can't count on being invited to dinner parties to meet new people. But should you manage to make friends with someone you've met on the subway platform at Grand Central Station and you begin to see this person for lunch or coffee, the relationship will probably remain at a certain level until one of you goes to the other's house.

There are millions of people out there who long for a better social life but just don't know exactly how to get there. Socializing is a learned art, one that I think is fading. We have forgotten many of the rules, methods, and techniques that constitute the friendship-building process. In this book, I offer practical strategies for every step of making friends—from first moves to maintaining a close friendship—including asking friends out for the first time, negotiating boundaries, when to invite people over, what kind of party to have, how to be a good hostess and a good guest, how to make a dinner party a success, rules for houseguests, how to handle sticky social situations of all kinds, and much more. Mostly this book is about communication and connection, and about truly enjoying the company of friends.

One of the best evenings I had with friends last year was not at a super-fancy restaurant, the opera, or a celebrity ball, but was a simple dinner party at the home of my friends Gary and Barbara. We had something delicious but simple to eat—salad with shrimp. The six of us around the dinner table that night were people who had been having each other over for dinner about once a month for eight years. These people had taken on the patina only old dining companions can have; our interaction was a rich tapestry of humor and familiarity created from cooking together, eating together, and talking about our lives—or just talking about nothing. That particular night, we spent about two hours discussing the differences in connotation between the word "jealousy" and the word "envy." We got out the *Oxford English Dictionary*, we argued good-naturedly, we shared stories from our own experiences. We ate and we laughed. We were adults at play, and the evening spun out like a dance performed by a couple who know each other well. Within this seemingly trivial conversation, we were really examining our lives, and redefining and relishing our relationships with each other. This was not a conversation you could have had in thirty minutes over coffee at Starbucks. The value of the dinner party is not about the quality of the food or the wine as much as it is about the hours you spend together *while* eating and drinking. I came away from that evening with a profound sense of contentment. I smiled for a week.

Alas, Gary and Barbara have since moved to Seattle. But I'm hosting a dinner party next Saturday and I've invited Susie. And guess who else is coming? Karl. I hope he knows he'll have to check his laptop at the door.

CHAPTER 1

The Best Life Is a Social Life

From the second we are born, we reach out for the warmth and security of other human beings. Call it a yearning for the womb, the breast, or a smiling face; imbedded in our DNA is an irresistible urge to connect. Human existence is intrinsically scary, and trapped inside our separate bodies and minds, all of us can feel alone from time to time. The sharing of our lives with others helps us to create meaning and gives us a feeling of security and of belonging. It is close personal relationships, more than anything else, that feed our hearts and souls—and make us happy.

Now, for the first time in history, it seems as though our ability—or our inclination—to lead authentic, vital social lives is regressing. Human beings have always been a species that likes to congregate. (Even Buddhists who go on retreats where talking is completely forbidden will usually do it as a group, in order to feel the comfort and harmony of being with others.) People have always sought out community, whether it be a geographical community or a group based on common interests. Since about 1970, however, membership in group organizations like bridge clubs, bowling teams, neighborhood associations, churches, and service clubs like the Elks and Kiwanis has been steadily on the wane. Group participation in general is way down. Reportedly there has even been a major decline in picnic attendance!

So what is happening to our social selves? Are we simply working too hard and have no time to hang out? It's certainly more than that. For one thing, there are more people living alone in the United States than ever before (26 percent of U.S. households) and more people are living away from their home towns, away from the friends and family that would serve as a social core. Most of us drive around in our individual cars, and sit in front of our individual computers or TVs. And why go to the neighborhood block party or to a lecture at the community college when you have three DVDs waiting for you and a pizza just a phone call away? The result: People are becoming more and more isolated.

We have definitely not stopped longing for fulfilling social lives. However, much of the time we unwittingly substitute faux connections for the real ones we so desperately seek. It certainly doesn't *feel* as though we lack company—since we are constantly inundated with the voices and faces of people talking to us from the TV, the computer, the radio, or our iPods. Just like a person consuming nothing but junk food with empty calories, we keep wanting more and more of it because we are not getting enough of the real thing. We think we are tuning in, but in reality we are tuning out.

Unplugging from the Matrix

Sally is this fantastically cool woman I've heard people talking about. She lives on a tropical island but visits the big city frequently. She is, by any standards, stunningly beautiful. She has cascading brown hair; a figure both men and women drool over; and tan, flawless skin. Always decked out in the latest Dolce, Prada, or Theory fashions, Sally is smart, funny, and proficient at all sports—she hang glides, swims, rides horses, skis, skydives, snowboards, and rappels. She even wins dance contests in her community's nightclubs.

The secret to her success? Sally is a computer-generated avatar.

We are living in an ever-intensifying world of virtual options—a world in which we can create our own digital 3-D personas and exist almost entirely in fantasy realms—inhabiting, exploring, and helping to build virtual communities like Second Life, Cybertown, and Active Worlds. We can have conversations, drinks, sex, or fights with people—all anonymously, and all online. There are an endless number of entertainment and informational experiences to be had in cyberspace. Any recorded fact (or factoid), photo, film clip, sound bite, song, or phone number is a mere keystroke away, as is every conceivable product or service. The Internet is one of the best people connectors ever invented: It's free, it's global, and it has no boundaries. Facebook, LinkedIn, Reunion.com, and other sites allow us to locate people we might never meet or reconnect with otherwise—at least not without hiring a private detective. But in spite of the Web's limitless power, it's important to remember that social networking is not necessarily the same thing as socializing. The truth is that we are spending way too much time online.

Believe me, I am not a Luddite. I just got a brand-new Nano, I check my e-mail twenty times a day, and I panic like crazy if I forget my cell phone. One day last week I couldn't get Internet service and was without e-mail for seven hours. I became a raving lunatic. I love and need the convenience and luxury of all my electronics. But when our relationship with technology gets to the point that it becomes more important for us to get our votes in to *American Idol* than to call up a friend, it may be time to push the Off button, if only for an hour or two.

Every generation has had its doomsayers, folks convinced that the latest invention or social trend heralds the end of the world as we know it. When jazz became popular at the beginning of the twentieth century, parents wanted to lock up their children; when the microwave oven was invented in the 1950s, the end of civilization was again predicted. So couldn't all this fear about the current technology explosion simply be this generation's version of the alarmism that almost always accompanies change? Maybe. But I think the real difference in the case of the computer (and, for that matter, all things with glowing monitors!) is the exponentially increasing amount of time we are spending with it.

In addition to the 2006 Nielsen report showing that the average amount of television watched by individual viewers in the U.S. is up to a record high of 4 hours and 35 minutes (with household viewing of more than 8 hours a day), surveys show that the average Internet user spends 3 hours a day online. The average twenty-year-old now spends at least 6 hours a day on the Internet—more than one third of his or her waking life. The computer tech support site Support.com reports that 65 percent of people spend more time with their computers than with their mates, not to mention the fact that the average person wastes 12 hours per month trying to fix home computer problems! More than 60 percent of office workers take their BlackBerrys or cell phones to bed with them. There are already many psychologists and sociologists studying what some are calling IAD: Internet Addiction Disorder. Some are concerned about the ways in which our brain functions are being altered by life on the Net.

Whether IAD is a real disorder or the psychological fad of the week, it is undeniable that people can and do develop dependencies on television, video games, and computers. However, unlike video games or even TV, computers have an intrinsically valuable function; that is, unless you are totally off the grid, they are essential to our daily lives. The problem is they actually make many things *too* easy. In a world when you can text the *New York Times* for the latest style news, receive stock quotes on your cell phone, or watch a live soccer game that's taking place on the other side of the planet, the real world can seem pretty tedious by comparison. Why bother going out and buying a newspaper? Why go to the trouble of trying to reach someone by phone—especially when IMing that same someone means you can quickly scroll to the end if he or she starts talking about something you are not interested in? In offices, people who used to get up and go into a neighboring office for a chat now just e-mail each other. It is fairly common to find coworkers just a few feet apart IMing each other instead of turning their heads to talk, and even typing "Hahaha" or "lol" rather than laughing out loud at each other's jokes.

I know I am certainly not the only person to wonder exactly where this escalation of dependence on technology will end. It doesn't take that much imagination to envision a future that looks like a sci-fi horror film: all of us sitting in our perfectly ergonomic Aeron chairs, alone in our cubicles with wires coming out of our heads, blinking our eyelids to point and click, and Fresh Direct robots delivering food to the door, which only gets opened to let in things, not people.

Okay, I admit this is probably a far-fetched scenario. We are not there just yet. But consider the rapidly expanding blogosphere.

The Blog Bog

Blogging is by far our fastest growing interpersonal arena. More than one in ten adult Internet users in the U.S. have blogs. Many people regularly read at least three or four blogs per day. The growing trend of voyeurism that has led fictional (or "scripted") TV shows to be replaced with "reality" shows is also fueling the narcissistic blogging climate. Not only can you now be the star of your own story—in blog or video diary form—but you can also completely surround yourself with your own subjective opinions mirrored in the blogs of others. What began as a talk radio concept—that is, ordinary people calling in and being given as much "journalistic" weight as the host—is now multiplied a million-fold in Internet blogs. Never mind the blogger's sources or what the hidden agendas might be. Techno-social interaction has turned everyone into an author, a publisher, a celebrity, and a paparazzo. It seems we are watching life and talking about life, not living life.

Notwithstanding the many news and political blogs, most people blog because they want other people to know about who they are and what they think. Part of the blogging phenomenon is sharing the details of one's personal life (and publishing them permanently) with the whole world. It would seem to be an attempt at intimate connection, even at the expense of privacy and dignity. But are bloggers really letting others into their lives? Isn't the kind of anonymity cyberspace affords actually the *opposite* of intimacy? Meanwhile, between blogging and YouTube and e-mailing and IMing, most of us can end up glued to the computer screen for the majority of the day. Though I know plenty of people will disagree with me on this, as much as I love my computer, I cannot truly be intimate with it.

Here is a little quiz to take to see if you might be in danger of becoming a cyber-junkie:

The Online-O-Meter

1) Do you find that your fingers move (as if typing) when you speak, even when you are nowhere near a computer?
2) Would you rather IM a friend while having a drink, or go meet that friend at the corner bar?
3) When you close your eyes at night, do you see a computer screen in your mind's eye?
4) When entering a friend's house, do you ask about the WiFi signal before saying hello?
5) Do you get irritable when someone interrupts you when you are immersed in cyberspace?
6) When you have sex with someone for the first time, is your first thought, "I wonder if this is the one I've been waiting for..." or is it "I can't wait to blog about this"?
7) Do you feel guilty about the amount of time you spend on the Internet, and want to cut down but can't?
8) Do you really, really want to put this book down right now and go online?

Please don't send the cyber-cops after me. I am not telling you to throw away your computer. And no, we have not really entered the world of *The Matrix* (not quite yet, anyway). But like the saying "Are you eating to live, or are you living to eat?" you just might want to ask yourself: "Are you on the Internet to connect with people, or are you connecting with people as an excuse to spend more time online?"

If you hesitate when answering, I would advise that you try to "unplug." (Not totally. That might be too much of a shock to your system. Just intermittently!) Remember: You are not socializing until you can get close enough to see the whites of their eyes—and smell their perfume.

iPod, You Pod, We All Pod

Speaking of unplugging, I often have to remind myself, when approaching the elevator in my building while listening to my iPod, to take the darn buds out of my ears when a neighbor speaks to me. Having a conversation with one of my neighbors is more important than anything I might be listening to, and it is just plain good manners to respond to this person—to connect for the few moments we are enclosed in this space together. After all, this is someone in my community. We need each other—whether it's because we both hate the landlord or because we are on the co-op board together. And though what I was listening to may very well turn out to be more exciting than what my neighbor has to say, my neighbor is a real flesh-and-blood human being and therefore takes precedence. It's even possible that talking to your neighbor instead of listening to your iPod will make a small difference in his or your day.

Remember the alien pod people in *Invasion of the Body Snatchers*? When I look at all the wires coming out of people's ears on the street, sometimes I feel as though we are all turning into iPod people! I admit that iPods make a crowded subway or torturous bus ride more endurable. However, whenever possible and whenever palatable, real life should always supersede recorded life. Here are some general guidelines:

You should remove your audio device from your ears when: 1) anyone speaks directly to you, 2) you go into a store or other public place to purchase something and you are nearing the cash register, or 3) you are eating at a table and you are not alone—that is, if you are acquainted with the people you are sitting with; in other words, when you are about to interact with a real live human being. Note:

Pulling out only one of the two ear buds is unacceptable. It gives the live person a sense they must compete with whatever is going into your other ear. You might as well close one eye.

Of course, iPods and cell phones are excellent tools if you are trying to dodge someone. (There are a couple of people in my building I won't unplug for if I can help it.)

Okay, take a deep breath. Unplugging can be uncomfortable at first. Like a fish out of water, you may feel awkward and flop around for a while.

Getting Addicted to Live People

Let me be perfectly clear. By "live people," I do not mean live video chat, Skyping, or live webcam broadcasts. (Computer video chats may make it seem like You Are There—but You Are Not!) What I mean is living and breathing, in-the-flesh people. Here's how you begin to get yourself hooked on real live people.

Although your ultimate goal is face-to-face interaction, you can lay the groundwork for your live person "habit" by occasionally picking up the phone when you would ordinarily send an e-mail. You will find that there are times a phone conversation is actually more efficient than an e-mail exchange (see page 62) In fact, this is true more often than you might imagine. If you work in an office, force yourself occasionally to get up and walk into a neighboring office for a chat instead of IMing the person. This will give you your initial buzz. But the hard stuff, the stuff of real addiction, will come when you get into the habit of talking to strangers. Talking to strangers—the very thing our mothers told us *not* to do when we were children—is actually extremely good for you.

Let's go. Put your computer to sleep (it's not Hal from *2001: A Space Odyssey*, so don't worry—it won't get mad at you) and go out and sit in a park or a café. Go to a nice restaurant and sit at the bar. Do this on your lunch break, or when you are at home on the weekends, or when you are going to and from your normal activities. Now, stop thinking about what you are going to buy at the market and what your husband said to you that annoyed you last night and just look around you. Notice what the person next to you is wearing. Notice what people are carrying in their arms or what they are reading. Listen to what they are saying. Feel their energy. Look for an opening and then—speak!

You may already be the gregarious type who loves to engage with anyone anytime. But if the idea of talking to someone you have never met seems totally bizarre to you, if you tend to be too embarrassed to talk to strangers—just push yourself a little and try it. Once you start doing it, you will really start to love it. You will get used to always talking to the person standing beside you waiting for the bus, the person in line in front of you at the supermarket. I myself can't get into a cab or an elevator without engaging in a conversation. Early on in my life, I made a habit of talking to strangers (sorry, Mom) and now I can't stop. I am absolutely hooked, and when I don't get it on a regular basis, I find myself pining for it.

You never know what interesting people you may meet if you just take the initiative. It sounds silly, but it could really change your life!

Last year my friend Frank found himself standing in a very long line at the Department of Motor Vehicles to renew his license. When the computers broke down and the wait went from tedious to exasperating, Frank decided to pass the time by talking to the person in front of him, a man named Henry. Frank learned a lot about Henry: his childhood in South Carolina, his college days at Harvard, his job as an IT professional at NBC. (And yes, Henry agreed with Frank—as thirty minutes of waiting became an hour—that computers could be a curse as well as a blessing.)

Four months later, Frank was on a train on his way to an important meeting in Boston—one that could make or break his career. He struck up a conversation with the man sitting next to him. It turned out that this person was a close friend of Henry's from Harvard! By the time Frank got to Boston, he had had such a good time and felt the coincidence was so amazing that it put him in a positive mood. Partially as a result of this experience, he totally aced the meeting (and also found out the best place to eat clams in Boston).

There are several different ways you can engage a stranger: You can ask for help or information ("How long have you been waiting for the bus?"), commiserate ("Can you believe how long this ticket line is!"), or make an observation ("Isn't it great that the heat wave is over?"). Remember, every person you come across in your life's journey is like a gift package waiting to be unwrapped. Every person is unique, with something special to offer. It might be a good something or it might not, but you'll never know what might be there if you don't open your mouth.

Warning: Don't go overboard. Talk to strangers too much without any sense of boundaries and you could end up at Bellevue with a Thorazine drip.

Overcoming Fears and Excuses

I've never met anyone who didn't feel lonesome or cut off at some point in his or her life. Whether it's because they've just left a long-time job, their best friend recently moved away, their children have gone off to college, or they are newly separated from (or frustrated with) a mate, from time to time, most people feel the need for more intimacy in their lives. Often a person will sense something important is missing even when there have been no major life changes. Loneliness is as common as the common cold.

Still, many people seem to be afraid to commit to the effort it takes to build lasting friendships. *Will it be worth it in the end,* they wonder, *or will I just waste a lot of time and still feel the way I do now?* Others think you either have to be actively looking for a spouse or looking for a job to get out there and socialize. And many are convinced their social lives are completely fine the way they are.

Not too long ago, I was talking to an old college friend about writing *Life is Friends.*

"What a dumb idea for a book," he said.

A horrible chill went up my spine.

"What do you mean?" I asked nervously.

"I have enough friends already," he scoffed.

I thought back to the month before, when this very same friend had been complaining bitterly about his life never changing, about each day being exactly like the rest. I started breathing again. My old college friend, like so many others, was denying his friend-making impulses and not even aware of how it was affecting him.

The impetus to make friends seems to fade when we get older. Almost everyone I talked to who is over forty has rationalizations for why they don't pursue new friends. But here's the secret I want to share: Socializing can be the best fun there is in life, better than sex (well, not better than really great sex). And like most things worth pursuing, the process is more important than the goal. In other words, it's not so much about having friends, it's about *making* friends, and about nurturing friendships. A good social life should not be static.

Most philosophers and spiritual leaders agree that there exists in us a basic conflict between fear and love, or fear and hope. Every emotion, impulse, or choice can be seen as coming from a place of either love or fear. Fear is staying home alone or being closed to the possibility of meeting new people. Love is meeting people and going out.

Of course, most people will never admit they are afraid to go out and try to make new friends. Instead they have excuses. Let's address the most common ones:

EXCUSE 1: *I don't need any more friends.*
It is true that there are a few extraordinary people out there who have so many really good, rich friendships that it takes most of their energy keeping up with them and they don't have a lot of leisure time left. But even these rare folks should keep their doors open. You might not have time to pursue every person who comes along, but to say "I have enough friends and don't want any more" is to say that you don't need any more love or laughter in your life. Think for a moment about the good friends you do have. What if you had missed the chance to get to know one of them? Exactly how many friends is enough? It's always possible that you have yet to meet the most amazing friend you'll ever have. (And you never know—one of your current friends could move to Timbuktu, leaving an opening in your social calendar.) For the most part, people use this excuse as a defense. It's like saying: "My life is perfect and there is no room for any improvement," when actually the opposite is true.

EXCUSE 2: *I'm too busy.*
I have had people tell me they are so overwhelmed by work and by the tasks of daily life that they have no time left for socializing.

How can they possibly justify going out to lunch when the laundry is not done and the screen door needs fixing?

My answer to this one is simple: Are you too busy for happiness? Too busy for love?

Being busy is the definition of modern life. *Of course* you are busy! But we still need to make the time for things that are important.

EXCUSE 3: *It's too hard. It takes too much effort.*
Putting yourself out there *is* hard. Hard in the same way that getting yourself to the beach and diving into a cold ocean is hard. But it is *so* worth it in the end. People who use this excuse are usually covering up a deep fear of change. Change is what life is all about.

EXCUSE 4: *It's too scary.*
Most people are plagued by social insecurities. They think: *I don't want to go because people will find out that I am a loser. I will be bored/ boring. I won't have anything to say. What if I like someone and they don't like me? I don't need any more rejection in my life. I would rather stay hidden and safe.*

These kinds of fears are the most straightforward but sometimes the hardest to conquer.

I met a handsome, successful man at a wedding brunch once. He was funny, nice—altogether charming—which was why at first I did not believe him when he confessed to me that he abhorred dinner parties. Unlike most people, he actually found going to small, sit-down parties more uncomfortable than going to large cocktail parties. It took some pressing, but I finally found out what the man was actually scared of: At a small sit-down gathering, where he was unable to escape those at the table, he thought others would find out he had nothing interesting to say. Of course, the irony of this personal disclosure was that my exchange with this man was by far the most interesting conversation I had throughout the entire brunch.

As FDR said, "The only thing to fear is fear itself." Even the wedding brunch man knew that he had a problem he needed to conquer. If he goes to enough dinner parties he will soon lose his fear because people will undoubtedly like him as much as I did.

Where to Fish for Future Friends

Now that you are ready to expand your social life, where do you look for these new friends? One thing is for sure: They won't come a knockin' at your door. They won't call you up out of the blue. You are going to have to go out and get them the way you would go out and get a job!

Computer Networking Sites
In spite of my warnings about virtual life, there are many good online avenues for meeting people. The important thing about this venue is to remember that your goal is face-to-face meetings. After you connect with someone interesting, get the relationship off the screen as quickly as you can. Many marriages are to the credit of online dating services, but that's because they are designed to help you meet in person. There are similar sites for platonic hookups; the best one—a wonderful use of the Internet—is Meetup.com. Meetup.com is basically a sign-up sheet for getting people together who share the same interests. This is social networking as it should be. So look for sites where you proceed quickly to one-on-one e-mailing, then face-to-face meetings. (Obviously you

will need to be careful when picking up strangers off the Internet. You can't always tell everything from e-mails. Don't meet in a dark alley—unless it is a bowling alley.)

In Public

I don't mean you should go stand on the corner and hand out your phone number to passersby, but you will find as you move through your life many places where you see the same people regularly. Over time, relationships can develop in places such as the grocery store, the library, the bookstore, the laundromat, the gym, the neighborhood pool, the local bar or coffee shop, and the train you take every day for work.

Years ago, I was called for jury duty. I was stuck on this horrible white-collar crime case—for seven weeks! And because we were not allowed to talk about the case, of course, a fellow juror—an actor named Ian—and I had nothing to do but go out to lunch every day and get to know each other. Now, I could have spent that time on the phone, or shopping, or working, but I decided that fate had put me in that courtroom, so I'd see what fate had to throw my way. Ian and I have been good friends for more than ten years now.

There is no village square in most people's lives in this century. However, people are becoming more aware of this need for our public spaces to provide viable social arenas. In fact, there are new real estate developments that are actually including sidewalks and community spaces. New apartment buildings are being built in urban areas which have "block party" spaces on every floor—places where tenants can hang out (in pajamas or in suits and ties) and eat breakfast with their neighbors. One new condo in Brooklyn named "Hello" has poker tables, rooftop cabanas, a barbecue area, and wine cellars to motivate people to fraternize. These progressive developments recognize the need that people have for socializing and are promoted with these features as building perks.

Hobbies/Pursuing Interests

Since the very first how-to book, people have been offering advice about taking classes, pursuing hobbies, or joining churches and clubs. It's almost a cliché by now. But clichés are clichés for a reason. These activities, while requiring a good deal of motivation, can open up your life enormously. For making new friends, there is nothing like a shared hobby. However, keep in mind that what you pursue should be something you really enjoy rather than something you do because you think you will meet the "right" kind of people. Making friends this way will only work if you are truly interested in the subject or event. So don't take a class in collecting antique cars because you think you will meet rich people; take it because you are truly obsessed with 1957 Rolls Royces.

Workplace

When you make friends from work, they are often friends for life. These are relationships that grow out of completing tasks and projects together. Working day after day in the same environment creates strong bonds. It is almost like sharing a house (but not quite). If you are lucky enough to find like-minded people at work, it's an easy place to make friends.

Some people, however, don't want to cross those boundaries. One woman I interviewed, Mary, was adamant about not making friends at work. It's not that there aren't nice, interesting people where she works, but she believes in total separation of work and home. "I need boundaries between work people and play people," she said. She told me the only way she can leave the stress of work behind is to have no crossover between her two lives. I, on the other hand, am still best friends with people I worked with in publishing twenty years ago. It just depends on who you are.

One thing is for sure: When scoping out friends at work, you can afford to (and you must) go very slowly. Keep in mind that whether or not the friendship develops, you still have to work together. The last thing you need is any awkwardness because of a bad platonic date. Also, be aware of the power structure or balance; if you are the boss, people may act as if they are your best friend when it's mostly about succeeding at the job.

Friends of Friends

The richest ore for friendship mining, the friends of your friends are like wonderful gifts. Because these new people are already "vetted" by those you love and respect, the likelihood of your finding common ground with them—of their being of like mind— is extremely high. But of course you have to have the help of your friends. As you get older, the friends-of-friends connection may become more limited, for various reasons. Especially in the city, people can be weirdly territorial and compartmentalized about this. Sometimes there are complications when worlds collide. But we will get into that later.

Socializing Versus Social Climbing

There is a difference between social*izing* and social *climbing*. That difference has to do with the kind of goals you have when you are meeting people. All too many people make the mistake of looking for friends who can further their career or their social standing. Please believe me when I say that you will end up much happier if you seek out people with whom you feel genuinely simpatico. If these people happen to be ambassadors, CEOs, or famous artists, so be it. But if you go for the cool people because you think they will look good on your mantle, you will end up with inauthentic relationships—or ones that don't stick.

This is not a black-and-white issue. For instance, you might have learned from experience that people who are artists tend to have tastes and values similar to yours, so when you find out someone is an artist it makes her a more attractive prospect. You might already be really enjoying talking to someone at a party and then, when you find out he is the New York Knicks' general manager, the power and glamour of his profession can make him even more desirable. That nice couple you and your husband have been sitting with during your kids' soccer practice may seem even nicer when you find out they summer in Provence—and they have a guest room. Successful people are often very interesting, compelling people. However, if you meet someone who you think is an insufferable, pompous ass, but after you find out he is the director of programming at NBC, you decide to pursue a friendship (which you really wouldn't have at all otherwise)—you, my friend, are a social climber. I interviewed a woman who confessed she had met a very interesting woman in the waiting room of her dentist, but that after she found out the woman worked as a secretary for Price Waterhouse, she lost interest. Don't be a snob. Your friends can come from anywhere.

Ask yourself: Are you searching for status friends or heart friends—people with whom you can be yourself? Life is too short to spend time with those whose company you do not enjoy. On the other hand, there is nothing wrong with social climbing per se. It can get you into important places with important people. It can get you a summer vacation in a villa in Spain or an office with a window. Just remember that it can't get you true friends.

Turning on Your Social Light

You can decorate the entire Christmas tree, the front lawn, and the whole house with as many colorful lights as will fit, but the desired effect only occurs when you turn on the electricity. Similarly, this entire chapter is only theory unless you have the right attitude to go with the advice. It may sound trite, but you have to get yourself in the right frame of mind, and that usually means changing the way you think about your social life. There will be a big part of you that feels as though your life is perfectly fine, thank you very much. You are going to have to shake yourself out of this kind of complacency. Other people will feel that their lives are not great but, you know, you can't fight City Hall, right? They might say, "I have no control over what happens. It may suck, but this is my life." If you feel stuck in the old stay-at-home-nothing-will-ever-change way of thinking, try the following exercises. (They may seem a little silly, but you don't have to tell anyone you have even read them, much less done them).

Mental Weightlifting

- Pretend you have just moved from another country and you will be deported unless you make friends.
- Pretend you are going to get paid for each new friend you make.
- Imagine that your soul mates from previous lives are out there, waiting to reconnect with you.
- Visualize spending more time laughing and smiling than anything else in life.
- Pretend you are writing a novel and everyone you meet is a potential character. In other words, study people. Listen to them. (Yes, eavesdrop. I give you my permission, as long as you are not using any electronic recording devices.)

Say Yes

This is the main thing: Go out. Go out. Go out. GO OUT. Go to lectures, go to rallies, go to events at restaurants and bookstores. Go to every party you are invited to. Go alone, go with your spouse, go with your kids, go with friends. Never turn down an invitation to anything unless you are already committed to something else or unless the invitation comes from a convicted serial killer. Especially be sure to go to any weddings or reunions of any kind you are invited to. I have actually turned down wedding invitations at various times because they were too far away; I always regretted it afterward when I heard about the experience. People bond big time at weddings.

One man, a classic minglephobe, told me a great story: He and his girlfriend were invited to a large cocktail party. She wanted to go; he didn't. He dug in his heels until finally she said to him, "I'll make a deal with you: If you go, I promise that we can leave in fifteen minutes. You just say the word."

He was dubious. "You absolutely promise?" he asked her. "Fifteen minutes and no more?"

"Yes," she swore.

They went, the minglephobe and his very, very wise girlfriend. And guess what? He had a wonderful time and stayed for the whole party. She practically had to pull him out the door to get him to go home. Once she had given him a foolproof "parachute" for a quick getaway, he was able to enjoy himself.

The reasons for always saying yes are that 1) it toughens up your social muscles and 2) life really can surprise you. I don't mean just because you might have a good time. You might meet someone who will become important to you.

I dragged myself to a neighborhood function one evening that I didn't feel like going to. I had had an unproductive day. I felt unattractive. I didn't feel like talking to anyone. Yet, I went (after all, I write books on this and I couldn't be a hypocrite).

The very first person I spoke to said to me, "Do I know you?"

After some tentative questions, we found the connection. We had gone to college together! We knew many of the same people. I would have said the chances of this happening were slim; New York is a very big city, it was a very small party, and we both grew up in other places and went to college in another state altogether. But that is the magic of these things. We now socialize regularly. She is one of my wonderful new friends.

Make meeting people a priority. Get ready, get set, and go social.

The Law of Attraction

We all want to attract people who will add to rather than detract from our lives. There is one universal truth that is wise to heed: the law of attraction. We tend to attract into our lives whatever we give attention to, whether positive or negative. In other words, what and whom you attract into your life is to a large degree a response to what signals you are sending out. If you have a rotten day, go to a bar with a bad attitude, and—because you are feeling bitter—drink too much, you are more likely to attract a negative sort of person than if you walk in feeling like a million bucks and thinking how sweet life is.

I know of a seventy-five-year-old single woman, a retired teacher, who gets invitations to everything all the time—weekends in the Hamptons, summers in Spain. The reason for her popularity is that she is a very positive, enthusiastic person, totally engaged and excited about people and life. People are attracted to positive energy the way they are attracted to a warm fire on a frosty night. It's really not about who is the nicest person, the most generous person, or even who is the best listener (although all those qualities help); it's about the power of positive energy. It is the thing most people want to be around. This does not mean you have to be a Pollyanna. It's okay if you feel depressed sometimes; that's not what I am talking about. It is more about how you interact with the world. (I never trust people who say they are happy all of the time. I think people who are constantly cheerful are usually hiding something underneath.)

I'm not sure whether the law of attraction works because of a physical energy, a psychic energy, or a psychological one, but believe me, it works. In fact, I find that if I am in a negative mood, my phone won't even ring. When I am feeling excited and connected to the world, it rings off the hook.

The best life really is a social life. The urge to socialize is like the urge to laugh; you may think you are perfectly happy not doing it until you start doing it and realize what you were missing. In the end of your life, it's going to be friends that matter. Open up your door, open up your life. Let people in. Don't just communicate, commune!

Ultimately you will want to start inviting more people into your home. But first, you have to make friends. And believe it or not, like many things in life, there is an art to making friends.

CHAPTER 2

Platonic Dating

A PLAYDATE PRIMER FOR GROWN-UPS

(Ringtone)
JOE: "Hello?"
BOB: "Is this Joe?"
JOE: "Yes?"
BOB: "I, um, this is Bob.
JOE: "Bob?"
BOB: "Bob Thompson. We met at Sally Smith's party last week..."
JOE: "Oh...I think...oh yeah! You were the guy who invited Jane and me to the housewarming? It's this weekend, right? We're really looking forward to it."
(Silence)
BOB: "I'm not...I mean...That wasn't me."
JOE: "Oh! Sorry. I thought...Who'd you say this was?"
BOB: "Um...*Bob*. Bob Thomson?"
JOE: "Oh, sure! Right! *Bob*. How the hell are you, Bob?"
BOB: "Er...Fine. How are you?"
JOE: "Glad to hear it...Good. I'm great!"

(Silence)
BOB: "Well, anyway, I don't know if you remember, but I have these season's tickets for the Mets and . . . well, I thought if you weren't busy on Friday, we could . . . "
JOE: "Friday? . . . Oh . . . Jeez . . . I'm sorry but I actually have plans that night."
(Silence)
BOB: "I guess that must be the housewarming."
JOE: "Well, actually . . . yeah." (nervous laughter) "I kind of feel like an idiot."
BOB: "No, of course not, don't worry about it. Well, okay. Well, it was nice to, er . . . "
JOE: "Maybe another time?"
(Silence)
BOB: "That's okay, man. Bye."
JOE: "Wait, I'm serious . . . A game would be great. I love the Mets!"
(Click)

Will Bob and Joe ever get together after their awkward beginning? Meeting a potential new friend is very much like meeting a potential romantic partner (even when the meeting is between two straight men). Like dating, making friends is like a dance, one that usually begins tentatively and then becomes more assured as it goes along. And just as in romance, with the prospect of a new friend there exists the possibility for an increase of fun and excitement, the promise of a more enjoyable life because of the addition of someone who gets you. But there is also a certain amount of trepidation involved. Even though a platonic encounter obviously lacks the intensity of romance, you are still putting yourself out there, taking an emotional risk. And sometimes it can break your heart almost as badly.

Civilization is a little under the weather when it comes to the niceties of social life. And while I am no Emily Post and I really don't care which fork you use or how you unfold your napkin, I do believe there are certain social structures and rules that aid us in our efforts to connect. This chapter will cover a few of the basics for succeeding in the realm of "platonic dating."

I know what you are thinking. You already know how to make friends; you've been doing it since childhood. Why would you need instructions? It should be as easy as when we had playdates as kids, right?

There are some people out there for whom this is entirely true, but not as many as you'd think. It's a funny thing about grown-ups; most of us acquire a lot of protective emotional layers along the way. And because we *are* adults, weighed down by adult baggage and busy with our adult lives, we need guidelines as we begin new friendships—just so that it all goes as smoothly as possible. We have limited time and energy, and one or two moments of unease or discomfort during an initial encounter may cause us to give up when we shouldn't.

If making friends is a dance, it's a dance that many of us have forgotten the steps to. Proceeding with the right skills protects you and the other person from awkwardness and rejection, and ensures that a budding relationship has a chance to flower—and a chance to enhance your life.

First Moves, or How to Say "I Like You" without Scaring Them Away

Testing the Waters

Imagine you are at a large barbecue given by a business acquaintance. After forcing yourself to mingle with several groups of strangers (a necessity, as you know very few of the guests), you've met a really nice, interesting woman named Marybeth. You seem to have a lot in common: you both have husbands but no children, you both love biking, and you both—coincidentally—grew up vacationing with family at the same beach town in New Jersey. You know you should probably keep circulating throughout the party, but you are having too much fun talking to Marybeth. She isn't making a move to leave, either. The two of you are laughing much more than you can ever remember laughing with someone you barely know. You're thinking that you are absolutely going to be seeing each other anther time, that you have found a friend. You are poised and ready to make a playdate with her—to "ask her out."

Hold on. Although Marybeth's behavior could very well mean she is ready to take the next step, this is not necessarily the case. She could be having a fine time talking to you, but not have any interest in seeing you again after this particular event. A lot of people will glom onto one person at a party, and it's nothing more than the minglephobe's lack of willingness to make their way through the crowd. Or it could be that they are just naturally charming to everyone, or they are in an uncharacteristically gregarious mood. It's a good idea to test the waters, to sort of stick your toe in and take the temperature before leaping all the way in. Asking someone out on a playdate too soon could cause you both embarrassment and ruin a nice time.

I have found that often the best way to proceed is with a test line—a kind of preliminary probe designed to see if you are both on the same page. Test lines are very much like romantic pick-up lines, though a platonic pick-up line is usually less overt than a romantic pick-up line would be. The responses you get will range from *cool* (I'm not interested in pursuing anything) to *warm* (you're somebody I think I could be friends with) to *hot* (I feel like I've known you my whole life!). Remember: It can be just as hard being rejected platonically as it is romantically. This is why you are going to go forward carefully.

Okay, you've replenished your Margaritas (which, naturally, you both like over ice with salt). You've just been talking about biking in the city. You decide to test the friendship waters with: "I've never been biking on that path. I'd really like to do that sometime."

Now, if Marybeth responds with, "I don't ride there that much anymore," and drops the subject, this is a *cool* response, and may indicate that she has no interest in seeing you again. (Note: A cool response is not a definite negative. She could have, in fact, stopped riding on the aforementioned path and is just being truthful.) If she responds with, "It's such a great path! I usually go on Sundays. You really should try it," this is a *warm* response. It's not quite a commitment, but it sounds as though she would like to run into you again. A *hot* response might be, "I'm going tomorrow at five. Why don't you come?"

Below are other sample test lines. You'll note that they are not in the form of a question. Questions can be too confrontational; you always want to allow the other person an easy out.

Test
"Like you, I totally love Woody Allen films! I can't wait to see the new one."
Response
COOL: "I haven't heard too much about it." (Full stop.)

WARM: "Me, too. Maybe we could go together sometime, who knows. Make sure I have your e-mail address before you leave."
HOT: "I would love to see that that. I'm busy next week, but the week after that looks good. Call me at work to make a date—I'm usually reachable in the mornings."

Test
"I've heard the new Peruvian restaurant on Main Street is unbelievable. I need to get down there before it's discovered and gets too crowded."
Response
COOL: "I dislike Peruvian cuisine."
WARM: "I know what you mean. In three weeks there will be a line around the block."
HOT: "Me, too—I have *so* been wanting to go to that place!"

If your new prospect is responding with either warm or hot—jump on in! The water's fine.

The Danger of Like-at-First-Sight
Sometimes it's so magical. It can feel exactly like when you were a kid and you met someone it seemed you'd known forever. You can't believe you found each other. You can already imagine the years and years of best friendship—growing old together, the dinners, the heart-to-heart conversations, weekends at country houses, your children (not yet conceived) going to school together...

Many dating books warn readers not to sleep together too fast. Similarly, in platonic dating you have to be careful that you don't go overboard at the beginning. The thrill of the encounter—the feeling of discovering a sought-for treasure of a person—may have you convinced that this new acquaintance is destined to be your best friend. In the first flush of friendship excitement, people are apt to get excited and say things like "You guys fish?! You *must* come up to our house in Maine!" but they might not really mean it when they wake up the next day.

Only time will tell whether or not you are going to be pals for life. This kind of "instant like" may indeed be a sign of a truly meaningful connection, a meeting of soul mates. But sometimes it can be a "false positive." (In our initial infatuation, we often project what we want to see.) So proceed with cautious optimism, not wild abandon. Not only may the other person's interest peter out, but also you yourself might realize, after getting to know the person better, that he really isn't your cup of tea after all. Keep in mind that it is much harder to extricate yourself if you have pushed the friendship along too quickly and have already seen each other ten times in one month.

Don't be overly impulsive in extending or responding to invitations the very first time you meet someone. If your new acquaintance asks you at the first dinner party to come and spend a weekend with her family in the mountains, wait for her to ask again. (Better yet, have lunch first.) Err on the side of restraint. Like love at first sight, like at first sight will not always bear the test of time.

Rejecting the Concept of Rejection

If you are playing poker, you can't win every hand. If you are actively dating (for romance), you probably reject many people after the first meeting. And if you are out there socializing for friends, it is inevitable that you will run into people who don't feel the same way you do and will not be interested in pursuing a relationship. (They will be busy all the time when you call them up to make a date, or they will let you know in some other way—hopefully not a mean one—that they do not want to be friends.) Try not to think of it as rejection. It's part of the process of finding your friendship matches. You will like people who don't like you, and others will like you when you don't particularly care for them. It's the way the dance goes. It has to be mutual; it's either a good fit or a bad fit. When someone spurns your platonic advances, move on. There are plenty of fish in the social sea.

The Half Date

Most of the time, people do tend to be somewhat guarded about "going out" with someone they have just met at a class, event, or party. You are basically strangers, after all. This is why the Half Date is the perfect first friendship step. The Half Date is just an extension of your first meeting; you simply take your conversation out of the class/event/party and go somewhere nearby for a drink, a cup of coffee, or a bite, right then and there. (If it is a party, you shouldn't go on the date until near the end so you are not rude to your host.) Because it is an add-on to something you were already doing, the Half Date doesn't feel as major as a separate playdate; it takes no commitment, no planning, no time to think too much about whether or not you really have the time and interest in seeing this person. If it's fun, it's easy to take the next step and see the person again. If it's not fun, it's easy to part with a "Well, it was so nice meeting you." A half date is just like a free sample. If you don't like it, there's no obligation to buy!

The Follow-Up

We all know how to do this in business, but it's one of those niceties in socializing that really makes a difference. Recently I made a new acquaintance at a dinner party—a woman with whom I had a long conversation at the dinner table and with whom I shared transportation home. After a week or so had gone by, she called me up just to tell me how nice it was to meet me and what a lovely chat we had had. This is a woman who knows that it is courteous to make a follow-up call that is just that and nothing more. She was not calling to make a date (though I'm sure I will get together with her soon). The follow-up call sets a good foundation for a friendship, and will often lead naturally to your first "playdate."

Basic Playdate Protocol

I am not going to go over every possible issue you can have on a playdate. Just remember—especially when you are just starting up a friendship—it is important to put your best foot, hand, and face forward. Each of you is bound to be hyperaware at the beginning, trying to figure out who the other person is and how well you are going to get along. You want as little awkwardness as possible. First impressions are very important; one or both of you may be thinking, "I think I like her, but what if I made a mistake about this person?" You won't want to be an hour late, unkempt, or inebriated on your very first get-together. Here is Miss Mingle's list of do's and don'ts for when you are just starting to "date" a new friend.

DO KEEP THE VENUE CASUAL. In the beginning of any relationship, it's best to stick to coffee, a drink, lunch, a casual dinner, or a movie. If you happen to have free tickets to a rock concert, it is probably better to take an old friend rather than someone you've only just met. Casual (and relatively quiet) venues are better for getting to know someone.

Do Communicate in Advance. A little pre-planning ensures there will be no mix-ups, no awkwardness about where you are going or who is paying. Even if it is not a first playdate, just a regular get-together with a friend you know pretty well, you will want to forewarn the friend if you have to be home by ten sharp, or if you will be bringing your pet boa constrictor. It's just being considerate. Pick the movie, restaurant, or other venue together, but try not to be either too pushy or too passive. If you are the one setting up the playdate, make sure you give the other person as much information as possible about the area, the restaurant, where to meet, etc. Note: Be sure to exchange cell phone numbers so that you will have a way of reaching each other if either of you is running late.

Do Call If You Are Going to Be Late. You must call as soon as you know you will be more than ten minutes past the agreed-upon time. Apologize sincerely, and if you don't have a good excuse, make up one. (In other words, "Sorry I'm an hour late; I couldn't decide what to wear," is not going to fly.) However, try hard not to be late at all. If you are chronically late, it says to others, "My time is more important than yours." And while narcissism may be the new black, believe me, it won't look good on you.

Don't Stand People Up. Ever. If you do—by some horrible chance—forget a playdate until the next day, I'm afraid this is an apology for Superman. It calls for an on-your-knees (figuratively speaking) apology and, if possible, flowers or a gift or favor as some kind as penance.

Do Reschedule When Canceling. When you cancel and it is for real (that is, you really do want to pursue the friendship but something unavoidable came up), make sure you offer to reschedule right then and there when you are canceling. Don't be vague about it or the other person may think you are trying to ditch them.

DO SPLIT THE CHECK. Don't let new friends pay for you—even if they have more money than you. Always split the bill. If you both had lunch, even if one of you had something more expensive than the other, try to split the bill down the middle. It's more convivial than counting pennies.

DON'T GET CARRIED AWAY WITH STORY-TELLING. We all tend to have stories about our lives that we like to tell. There are some personal experiences we feel define us, and we think if the other person knows the story it will somehow speed up the friendship. This is okay if the story is pertinent, but don't focus on it to the detriment of the conversational flow. And be sure you are really listening to the other person—and not just waiting to talk.

DON'T SHARE TOO MANY INTIMATE DETAILS. Don't tell every single personal detail of your life during your first several playdates; there will be time for sharing later. If the relationship fails to develop into something substantive, you will be happier you didn't spill all your guts right away.

DON'T GOSSIP ABOUT PEOPLE YOU BOTH KNOW. This could be tempting, when you are looking for things you have in common to talk about, but don't do it. You do not really know the person sitting across from you very well yet, and gossiping is always dangerous.

It's Not a Business Meeting: Conversation as a Leisure Activity

Breathless from a busy day, I arrived at the appointed time for my drink date. My friend John was already waiting for me. We hugged and ordered Happy Hour draft beers.

He smiled and said, "Shall I go first?" He then proceeded to tell me the latest news about his work, his family, and his new apartment. I love John and he is a dear friend, but he does have a habit of conducting our get-togethers like business meetings. Usually, after he has briefed me about his week for about fifteen minutes, he will lean back and say, "Okay, so tell me about you." And so I do, but it always feels a little as if we are in a conference and we are taking turns presenting reports.

A conversation should be like a good game of tennis—a true back-and-forth event. What you say should be influenced by the other person's reaction, and the conversation should travel naturally to where it wants to go. You mustn't try to control it—at least not altogether; you have to let it be what it will.

Obviously, you will both have a mental agenda—a list of things in your head that you want to be sure to tell your friend. But even if you have a limited amount of time, try to just enjoy the other person. Of course, if you have a problem that is weighing heavily on your mind, you may need to focus on that. But if you don't completely catch up with every single detail of your job, your kids, and so on, that's okay. Exchanging personal statistics is the missionary position of conversing; why not be more creative? Adults need to relax their minds the way children do and play a little more.

It seems silly to offer instruction on conversation, but considering the cyber state of communication these days, some of us may need a refresher course. Here are just a few pointers:

PICK THE RIGHT SUBJECTS FOR THE RIGHT PEOPLE. Not everyone is fun to talk politics with. Not everyone is going to be jazzed when talking about your trip to Tibet or how you slept with your masseur. Not everyone likes to laugh at silly puns. If you were playing cards, you wouldn't insist on playing bridge with a poker player. Find the conversational area that works for you both.

DON'T QUIZ THE OTHER PERSON TOO MUCH. If your conversation is overly punctuated with questions like, "You know, of course, the well-known writer Louis Begley?" or "Do you know the Rue de Seine in Paris?" pretty soon the other person, beginning to feel ignorant, may start lying and saying "uh-huh" rather than admit he doesn't know. This takes the blood out of a conversation because one of the participants is now slightly on his guard.

REALLY LISTEN. WITH ALL YOUR MIGHT. Make a space in your brain and let the other person's words in there. If you are really listening, your own responses may come out sounding new and exciting even to you. Most of us have canned phrases—things we say to people because they get a good reaction—and we are always searching for a place to slip them into the conversation. Try to be spontaneous instead.

Rules and Regulations for the Group Outing

Group playdates are great fun and are a close cousin to at-home socializing, which is ultimately your goal. Here are some quick rules for getting together in groups of three or more:

RULE 1: *Let everyone know beforehand it is a group outing!*
It's not fair to invite someone to the movies, and then when they get there you spring it on them: "Oh, I invited five of my other friends. Hope you don't mind." The group you have decided to gather together could be highly compatible and great fun, but you still must let all the participants know in advance. People have a right to decide what kind of evening they are going to have.

RULE 2: *Be a benevolent dictator.*
Someone has to organize the group, and if you are the leader, good for you for taking the initiative. But make sure everyone has a say in what you are doing and where you are going—at least they should have veto power. It's better to e-mail everyone and say, "Let's all go to dinner on Thursday. How about Marcello's on Sixth Street?" than "I've decided we should have dinner Thursday. Be at Marcello's at 8:15."

RULE 3: *Split the cost.*
With very few exceptions, the best thing is to split the bill equally among those present. If you are good at math and you have organized the group outing, you should be in charge of splitting the tab. But have pity on the couple at the end of the table who had nothing to eat or drink except coffee and cake; try to adjust so they don't get stuck with a $100 tab.

RULE 4: *Don't pair up.*
Try to not pair off for too long, conversationally. Think of the group as an orchestra. You can have a duet for a while, but for the good of the group experience as a whole you need to mix it up. (Also, don't monopolize the table, even if you think you are the wittiest one there.)

Proper Use of Your Communication Technology

I often wonder as I call (or text) someone from the bus to tell them I am running late for the movie, what did we ever do before cell phones? Never before has communication been so streamlined—so potentially super-efficient. It's almost impossible to lose each other, or to be in the dark about anything.

Computers and smartphones keep us in more constant touch with a greater number of people than we ever imagined possible. Often when I am working on my laptop, something will remind me of an old friend, perhaps someone I haven't spoken to in years, and—abracadabra!—I can send her an e-mail and our friendship can be instantly rekindled, just like that. This effortless back and forth feels almost like telepathy. Our electronic devices are invaluable when fostering new relationships, allowing us to make small, safe overtures. But they may also be making us socially stupid. Too many of us do not use these wonderful tools correctly.

Essential E-Mail Etiquette

There have been several books published on this subject, and there will undoubtedly be more. But here are what I believe are the most important issues:

The Unanswered E-mail

This may be my biggest pet peeve. It is unfathomable to me that there are people who will often fail to respond to an e-mail from someone they know. Question: How much time does it take to press the Reply button upon reading an e-mail to type in "Great!" or "Talk to you later," or "Wow . . . Sounds intense," or "Thanks!"

Answer: Less time than it took me to type this sentence. The notion that it is somehow okay to not answer an e-mail that clearly requires a response is part of a societal sickness—a social disease that I wish they could find a cure for.

For instance, what can a person be thinking when a friend e-mails and asks a question, like, say, "Did you hear about my brain operation?" and that person fails to send back a reply? What is it about the nature of e-mail that separates the message from the sender so much that it makes us lose all sense of decorum?

An acquaintance of mine recently went to the trouble of scanning and then e-mailing some twenty-year-old photos to a dozen or so college friends who were in the photos. Only one in five people wrote back to her to say they enjoyed these forgotten images from their past. All that is necessary in a situation like that is a quick: "Gee whiz! We sure were young!" And yet not responding has become so much the norm that no one thinks twice about it. Of course, many people receive so much e-mail they are overwhelmed by it. But if your in-box is so swamped that you lose track of e-mails, you must find some kind of system to prevent that from happening.

The rule: Especially when it comes to new friends—and whether it takes you an hour or a day or a week—you *must* respond to an e-mail. (If you are away and don't have access to your e-mail for more than a week, it is advisable to set up an auto-reply that says, "I am away and will respond when I return." And then make sure you eventually respond.) Failing to click on that Reply button may just cost you a friend.

Beware of the Reply All Button and Other Common Mistakes
On the other hand, there are people who reply *too* much. The Reply All button, invented primarily for the convenience of

interoffice communications, has caused more faux pas than anything in all of faux pas history. Let's face it: We have given up a lot of privacy in exchange for the efficiency of computer communication. Many people seem oblivious to the fact that when e-mailing, you are basically making an indelible electronic record that can be forwarded anywhere. The indiscriminant pressing of Reply All causes many of us to see information we simply shouldn't see. This can cause hurt feelings, embarrassment, confusion, or worse. If you were writing a letter to someone, would you go out and Xerox copies and send it to everyone you know?

One of the well-known flaws of the e-mailing process is that it encourages us to do everything at high speed. The Reply button is, diabolically, right next to the Reply All button. Before e-mailing, think to yourself, *Who is going to see this?* Check the address line in your outgoing e-mail: Are you sending it to the right person or people? If it is a group e-mail, is it really appropriate for every person on the list? Does everyone on the list really need to see a comment or response that is directed to only one of the group? Once you click Send, it's too late.

Regarding the ubiquitous group e-mail—whether it be a petition for a worthy cause, a joke, a chain letter, or a message from the Dalai Lama—be aware that many of us do not take kindly to having our e-mail addresses shared with the entire universe. Learn how to use your BCC (blind carbon copy) function; otherwise, it's as if you had written all your friends' phone numbers on the bathroom wall. If I have just given out my e-mail address to a new person in hopes of becoming friends and that person sends me a chain e-mail, I have a hard time not writing him off my list.

Hijacking a friend of a friend's e-mail address from a group e-mail is a common practice and acceptable if it's a small personal mailing. That said, it is considered poor form to pull contacts from someone else's mailing list. If someone sends out a change of e-mail address notice to her entire address book, you should not e-mail one of the other recipients, unless you already know the person.

The Surprising Value of Emoticons

Because I am a writer, when I first entered the e-mail world I prided myself on never using those insipid-seeming, simplistic symbols that were supposed to convey the tone of the missive. Certainly, I told myself, a good writer need not resort to these graphic aids. But that was before I sent my sister-in-law a joke about my brother that I thought was dripping with irony but that she took seriously, and as a result was mad at me for a week. And then there was the time I got an e-mail from my friend Jimmy asking why I hadn't invited him to my Fourth of July party, and I was filled with horrible guilt until I realized he was only kidding. (He had told me months before that he was going out of town, and that's why I hadn't invited him.)

I have come to believe not only that we should utilize these "e-mail condiments" but that we need more of them. We need better ones. I wish there were a symbol for irony, one for sarcasm, one for "just punning," and one to indicate crying laughter. It's so easy to misunderstand simple smiley faces and winks and the other clunky punctuation marks.

(P.S. Will someone please explain to me what the "tongue-out" symbol means?)

When It Is Better to Phone

In socializing, e-mail is perfect for quick exchanges of information ("The movie is playing at the State Theater at either 7 or 9"); what could take ten to fifteen minutes on a phone (calling, leaving a message, then the inevitable chitchat accompanying the information exchange) takes about ten seconds with e-mail. It is also wonderful for times when you want to choose your words carefully—when you are afraid that during a phone call you might slip up. However, there are many times people use e-mail when they should use the phone instead. For example:

· When you need to negotiate a playdate, that is, decide together on a movie, restaurant, or other details. One phone call can expedite what can take six or seven e-mails back and forth. You could iChat the information exchange, but keep in mind that being able to hear the sound of the voice greatly increases the ease of communication. (You'll be able to discern if the other person really wants to eat Ethiopian or is merely being polite). The phone is preferable.

· When you have news of serious import (a promotion, a marriage, a death, a birth).

· When you need to cancel a long-standing date. If you are already good friends, you can certainly cancel by e-mail. However, for new or new-ish friends or acquaintances, it's much better manners to use the phone. (For one thing, the person on the other end of your "cancel" needs to hear the sound of regret in your voice.)

· When you need to apologize for hurting someone's feelings. You might be tempted to take care of this by e-mail, but trust me, if the person's feelings are already hurt it is all too easy for that person to take your e-mail in just the wrong way—thereby exacerbating whatever problem you already have.

· When you are mad at someone. Trying to sort out emotional conflict by e-mail is like trying to put out a fire with a bucket of gasoline.

Phone-etics

According to my father, my grandfather used to answer the telephone with a loud, abrupt, "What d'ya want?" instead of "Hello." He considered the ringing of the telephone an intrusion into his home; he believed the phone was for making calls, not receiving them. Today, with most people having both land lines and cell phones—and using smartphones for calling, texting, e-mailing, and Web browsing—phones have become more like extensions of our brains than simple talking machines. But let's go over a few socializing rules for talking on the telephone.

Returning Phone Calls

Like e-mailing lapses, not returning phone calls is one of the signs of the end of the world. (And I am only sort of kidding.) Obviously, if you don't know the person (a salesperson, a poll-taker, a fan, someone collecting money for a good cause), you can get away with not calling them back. You can also choose to e-mail a person instead of phoning. But otherwise you cannot simply stick your head under the pillow of life and pretend it didn't happen. We are living in a society here, people! I don't care how busy you are, or how awkward returning the call may make you feel. Rules of courtesy exist for a reason. It may seem like a small thing, but there is not much distance between failing to return a phone call and failing to pick up trash you have left on the beach. Pretty soon we will be living in a dirty place where we are all rude to each other. Return the call when you think the person may not be home if you must, but do return it.

Caller ID: A Gift from Heaven

I signed up for caller ID years ago when I was ghostwriting a book for an impatient billionaire who would call me at all hours. Caller

ID changed my life; I felt as if I had discovered plutonium. It's well worth the price, as you will never be surprised by an unwanted caller ever again. All cell phones have this feature and eventually no land line will be without it, either. Of course, it does take a lot of the fun out of answering the phone. You never have that "I wonder who it could be" excitement you now see only in old movies.

Tip: Even though people may suspect you have caller ID, don't pick up the phone and say knowingly, "Hi, Jeanne." Just say, "Hello?" the way you normally would. It's off-putting to address someone before saying hello. The caller feels as if she has somehow been caught.

Call Waiting: Invention from Hell

I know that people with kids have to have call waiting (what if there is an emergency while they are on the phone?), but I still can't help thinking it is one of the rudest, most intrusive things ever invented. Particularly obnoxious is the person who calls you up, rousing you from whatever it is that you were doing, and then halfway through his first sentence says, "Can you hold on? It's my other line." (Hold on? Why don't *you* hold on while I hang up!) And anyway, didn't civilization somehow get along without call waiting for, like, 2,000 years?

However, if you do have call waiting, you must follow these two essential rules:

RULE 1

If you telephone someone, and your call waiting clicks in, say to Person #1: "Oh, I am *so* sorry, I need to check my other line, I'll be right back." And then—and this is the important thing—come back to Person #1 immediately. (Tell Person #2 you are on the other line and will have to call him back. Yes, even if it's long distance.) Only in an honest-to-God emergency is it acceptable to ditch Person

#1 for Person #2. Or if Person #2 is calling from another country (long, long distance).

RULE 2

If you are waiting for an urgent call and Person #1 calls you, say that you are very happy she called but are waiting for a call that you must take when it comes in. With this pre-warning you may, if said call from Person #2 comes, politely end the call with Person #1.

Of course, call waiting is a great dodging tool. If you get a call from someone you don't want to talk to, you can use the pretense of Rule 2, and just fake the call. But don't make the mistake of ever telling *anyone* you have ever done this; you will be amazed at how many people have a hidden streak of paranoia in them.

Voice Mail Mores

"Hello, Tracey, are you there? Oh, I can't *believe* you're not home . . . I was calling because, well—I know I probably shouldn't leave this on your machine, but . . . you will *never* guess who I ran into . . . Oh, stop it Dougie, Mommy's on the phone! . . . Dougie! Put the hairdryer down; your brother doesn't want his hair dried. No, I don't care what kind of smile he has on his face . . . PUT IT DOWN!! . . . Sorry, Tracey . . . Anyway, I ran into Tom on the street and he was with that new boyfriend of his, God is he cute . . . Why are all the cute men gay? . . . And anyway Tom told me I should be sure to tell you that—" *(Click.)*

Having someone's voice mail cut you off is a sure sign you are leaving a bad message. Don't pick up the phone when you haven't thought out what you are going to say if you don't get a live person. Keep it brief. The other person's voice mail is not the place for your audio autobiography.

Also, you must actually utilize your own voice mail system. You should not be compulsively picking up the phone every time it rings. Whether you are at home painting the ceiling, sitting in a café chatting with a friend, or in an important business meeting, if you suspect the call you are receiving is not urgent and you are engaged with something or someone else, let your voice mail take a message. You should return the call when you can give proper attention to it—when you are not risking rudeness to the people around you. I can't believe how many times people answer my phone call with a whispered, "I can't talk right now! I'm doing something important!" and then hang up. Voice mail is our friend. Use it.

The Cell-Phoniness of Modern Life

The invention of the cell phone is to social life what the invention of the automobile was to travel. It changed everything. Unfortunately, along with having the ability to let people know we are late or tell our stockbrokers to buy immediately, we also have developed what I call Lazyphone Syndrome. This ailment is the result of our always being reachable. For instance, why make a shopping list when you can just call your wife from the grocery store and discuss at great length what is on the shelves? Or, if you make a plan to meet someone at an art exhibition, why bother setting up a specific place and time, when you can just call each other when you get close to the museum? What starts out seeming like an efficient way to operate ends up being incredibly inefficient, by the time you both call each other six or seven times. ("Where are you?" "Over by the gift shop." "The gift shop? But I'm in the gift shop." "Wait, not the big gift shop—I'm in the small one ... Hold on, I'm getting another call ... ") If you had just set a time and place in advance, you could have had one conversation about it, and then spent the rest of your time actually looking at the art. In addition to Lazyphone Syndrome, many people have ADD (Adult Dialing

Disorder). Even when they are not getting a call, they must make one or text someone. ("Hi. wher r u? I m in MOMA. yes it's cool but have not looked at art yet.")

What this means is that more and more, people are not ever experiencing life where they are, as they are usually half connected to someone somewhere else.

My rules for cell phones are similar to my rules for iPods:

1) Never talk on the phone while you are interacting with a live person—unless that person has an interest in that cell phone conversation (for example, when all three of you are trying to decide where to eat). Okay, I know this is impossible—you can't really achieve it, but you can try. If your kid or husband or boss calls while you are out on a playdate with a friend, talk to them as briefly as possible and then hang up. Turn off your phone whenever you can. And whatever you do, try not to have that fight with your wife right there on the cell phone. Say, "Talk to you later, honey, my battery is low," if you must.

2) Don't have long calls on your cell phone when other people in close vicinity are not on phones themselves.

3) Always put your phone on vibrate when you are inside a private home or in a restaurant or café.

4) Whenever it's just as easy to call as it is to text, call. You get the warmth of a human voice, and a much higher quality conversation.

5) Don't call a friend from a cab—or any other place where you know you only have five minutes—and start an important conversation that you will inevitably have to cut short. ("Jill? How are

you? How is the divorce going? Oh, gotta go, the cab is pulling up to my stop.") These conversations should always begin with, "Hi. I'm in a cab, so I only have a second. Can I call you later when we have more time?"

6) I can't believe I even have to say this, but after watching in horror at one Christmas party as a man actually ate from the buffet table while talking on his phone, I suppose I must: Do not talk on the phone while you are mingling at a party—not unless you are trying to keep people away from you.

Tried-and-True Techniques for Artful Dodging

In an ideal universe, we would all like each other equally; we would all automatically be invited to everything. Saying no to someone would be as uncomplicated as saying no to more peas at the dinner table.

But let's be honest: Life isn't like that on this planet. There are going to be many times when we are approached by someone who wants to spend time with us and we are sure, for one reason or another, that we have no interest in pursuing a friendship with them. Maybe you've gone out a few times and realize it's not going to work out, or maybe you've only met once. Life is short. You have to be able to say no and not feel guilty. If you are going to get up the gumption to go out and talk to strangers, join in, take classes, and mingle, you are going to need to have some defensive techniques handy or you will end up doing things you don't want to do. You don't want to let your nervousness about rejecting someone keep you from getting out there, so let's make sure you are equipped with the proper dodging tools.

The word "dodging" has gotten a bad rap. It smacks of cowardice, of moral turpitude. But the fact is, good dodging is not only necessary to your social happiness but is, when done well, an act of largesse. Always remember that the purpose of this kind of dodging is to keep from hurting people's feelings. Many people are uncomfortable with lying—even white lying. But I am of the opinion that it is far better to sacrifice one's own comfort for the other person's, whenever possible. If someone asks you to a concert, isn't it better to say "Thank you *so* much for inviting me, but I am sorry to tell you I am already committed for that evening," rather than "I just don't feel like it"?

The Elegant Old-Fashioned No

Of course, if you can pull it off, the simplest thing to do is to say, "It's so nice of you to ask me, but I'm afraid it's impossible for me right now." And then say no more. Smile, be as nice and as polite as you can, but don't offer any excuse. This is the way they used to do it in the old days, the days when there were universally understood boundaries, chivalry, and strict rules of etiquette. A polite no would be enough, and it would have been considered the height of rudeness for anyone to ask you for further explanation. However, if—in today's less genteel world—the person whose invitation you've declined is audacious enough to demand a reason, you can always say, "I can't really get into it" or "I'm afraid we're busy." Or even: "My social life is out of control these days. I am very sorry."

The Missing Business Card

Having a person suspect you are dodging her is almost always preferable to that person suffering the embarrassment of a blunt rejection. So the next time you are at a party and someone you are definitely not interested in asks you for your card, your best course of action may be to tell her you have lost/forgotten/ run out of cards, and then—ask for hers. Of course you won't be using her card, but never calling her is a lot more gentle a rebuff than having to say no when she calls you.

The drawback of this maneuver is that you do have to be quite certain that the object of your dodge does not see you giving your card to someone else later. An after-the-fact, "Oh, look—I found them!" is not going to really cut it.

The Duck-and-Cover

An evolutionary descendent of primitive man's fear/response instinct, the Duck-and-Cover (otherwise known as the Crouch-and-Run) is a good way to deal with an unwanted overture when you are caught off-guard. The "duck" is a delaying tactic; the "cover" is your alibi. Here is how it's done:

STEP ONE: *The Duck*

You are lying on your couch watching TV. The phone rings. Because you are in a *Jeopardy*-induced trance, you pick it up without thinking twice. Unfortunately, the moment the voice says "hello," you realize it's that woman you met at the New Year's Eve party when you both had too many Bloody Marys and you had given her your number. She's going to want to have lunch and it's the last thing you want to do.

The goal of Step One is to delay, to buy time so that you can come up with a plausible out. Never show dismay at her calling; it will all go a lot more smoothly if you can throw her off the scent with an enthusiastic greeting ("Oh, hi there!"). Then go right into the duck:

"Listen, I'm just taking something out of the oven—I'll call you back in ten minutes." Now—and this is crucial—get the phone number and hang up immediately. Don't allow any space for further conversation. You need time to think up an excuse.

Other Sample Ducking Lines:
- "Wait, let me switch to a better phone."
- "Someone is in my office right now—can I call you back?"
- "I just got out of the shower and I'm dripping wet."
- "Right now I've got glue (ink/paint/grease/flour) on my hands."
- "I've got a kid here running around with no diaper on."
- "I was just walking out the door."

STEP TWO: *The Cover*
Okay. You've succeeded in making life stand still for a moment. Now you've got to come up with a "cover," an excuse that will allow you to say no while saving the other person's feelings. Before committing to a cover, be sure to consider carefully to whom you are going to tell this lie (or half-lie) and exactly what kind of access they have to your life. In other words, how easy will it be for them to disprove your lie later? If you tell Ms. Bloody Mary you can't have lunch because you are moving to another city, better be sure she doesn't work around the corner from you. The best excuse for someone you never want to see again is that you are going to be overwhelmed for a long time because of a work or family issue, and that you will try to call her when things settle down in a month or two.

Note: When fibbing, always stay as close to the truth as possible. It's hard enough to remember your real life; you don't want to have to remember too many details from a fabricated one.

While the Duck-and-Cover is ideal for handling telephone surprises, it can also be performed in face-to-face situations. You use the "duck" to remove yourself from someone altogether or at least for a few minutes. (If you are on the street, you can run off to catch a bus or say you are late for a meeting; if you are in a room together, pretend your phone is vibrating and go off to take an important phone call.) Then you call or e-mail with an excuse.

Passing the Dodge

This is that handiest of all staving-off techniques, otherwise known as the I-Have-to-Check-with-My-Wife ploy. Perfect for pop invitations, this dodge was ingrained in most of us as children ("I have to go ask my mother"). It's a bit of a dirty dodge, but it delays—like the duck-and-cover. This excuse also allows for the possibility that you may eventually accept the invitation—or that you will "forget" to check with your wife (husband/boyfriend/boss/cat-sitter) at all, thereby letting the whole thing dissipate.

Hedging Your Bets:
The Safe Way to Play a Dangerous Game

"Hedging a bet" is a sports betting term referring to the practice of betting on more than one winner so as to lessen the chances of losing. In socializing, hedging your bets—keeping more than one person on the line for a date—must be done with the greatest care. I know certain people who have no compunction in telling you that they "don't know what they are doing yet" when you inquire if they are free on Saturday night. This is *totally* unacceptable as a response, as it is tantamount to saying, "I have to wait to see if something more desirable comes along and if it doesn't maybe I'll do something with you."

No one talks about it, but almost everyone has different levels of friends: an "A" list, people who you really can't wait to see because it is with them you have the most fun; and the "B" and "C" lists, people who are nice to hang out with but who you aren't as excited to see. And I would be lying if I said that I had never tried to hedge my bets, when, for example, a friend asked me to a movie and I thought I might be invited to a dinner party, but the date for the dinner was not yet set.

If you are going to hedge, you can never let the person you are putting "on hold" know that she is, in fact, your second (or third) choice for the evening. As in good dodging, the fabrication of a white lie here is a kindness to the other person. "I may have out-of-town guests that weekend, but they haven't confirmed," is a good one, or "Oh shoot, I've tentatively been asked do something, but I'm not sure if the plans are going to work out or not. Would it be okay if I called you closer to the weekend? Naturally, I will understand if you need to make other plans." The best and easiest one is to say you have to check with your spouse (though of course you must have one).

Note: For the most part, best friends don't need to hedge or dodge. That's what's so good about intimacy. It decreases the need for fudging the facts. One best friend can say to the other, "Oh my god, I've just been invited to the opera! Do you mind if we reschedule our movie date?"

Guidelines for Pursuing Platonic Friendships Between Men and Women

In spite of what Harry says in *When Harry Met Sally* (that men and women cannot be friends because one of them always wants to sleep with the other), friendships between men and women can be deep and life-sustaining. But they can also be tricky. There are slightly different rules when you are having a platonic relationship where there exists (at least officially) the possibility of a romantic one. Obviously, the following can also apply to friendships between two lesbians or between two gay men.

If You Are Single and Your Friend Is Single

The main thing to keep in mind when you are socializing with someone whom you are absolutely not interested in romantically is that the other person might be *telling* you that he just wants to be friends but secretly would like something romantic to develop. Therefore it is important to be clear about your platonic-only intentions. Don't fall into the danger zone of flirting with the other person because it's fun or because you think he likes it. Whenever you can, even if you have to make it up, talk about other people you are seeing romantically. And use one of the following statements if you think he is getting the wrong idea:

- "This is a social gesture, not a romantic one."
- "Aren't you glad we aren't romantically involved?"
- "I'm so glad to be friends with someone who..."

If You Are Single and Your Friend Is in a Couple

This is easier for the other person, but could be harder on you—and you have the spouse to consider. It is to be hoped that your friend will set good boundaries, and will take care to be clear with both you and his spouse about his friendship with you. However, while it is not your job to protect their relationship, you do want to protect your friendship, so be sure to encourage the inclusion of the spouse in your get-togethers whenever you can. Always be even nicer to the spouse than to your friend if possible. Share with the spouse details about your own romantic dates; make sure the spouse knows you are out there dating. The success of these relationships really depends on the friend's spouse being cool and the couple's relationship being solid. At the first sign of your friend's affection for you turning sexual, back away. (Unless you want to have an affair. But that's another book.) As your friendship becomes more intimate and your friend starts telling you about the problems in his marriage, lend a sympathetic ear but *never* dis the spouse.

If You Are in a Couple and Your Friend Is Single

If it's you who is in the couple, bring your friend and your spouse together as much as you can, and try not to complain about your spouse to your friend. Triangles are relationship minefields. However, you should also make an effort to not gloat too much about having a mate. Be sensitive to your single friend's lack of partner. Going on and on about how wonderful it is to be part of a couple is not being a good friend.

If You Both Are in Couples

This is obviously the easiest configuration. You are both already romantically involved so the boundaries are clear-cut. You will probably socialize much of the time in couple formation, though that can have its own difficulties. For example, it's rare that the spouses like each other as much as you and your friend like each other. Moreover, if one of the couples breaks up it can wreak havoc on the friendship (see page 247).

What to Do When You Have Romance in Mind

If you do feel romantically inclined toward a new friend, you need to get the relationship out of the platonic realm ASAP, like—fast! So when the guy you are interested in leans across the table from you and says, "It's so much fun to have a woman *friend!*" better do something drastic, or soon you will be helping him deconstruct his dates the morning after. In most cases, you have a limited time to make it sexual before you are permanently living in Platonic Land.

Be sure the object of your lust knows how you feel. Try to do "couple" things. You can make a concerted effort to flirt (there are lots of books and articles out there on flirting), but you'll mostly just need to let nature take its course. Many people swear by certain kinds of arm and/or knee touching while maintaining eye contact. You could use the traditional route: Wear something sexy and get him tipsy. "Pounce" (i.e., plant a hot kiss on him) if you can, though pouncing is still often easier for men (I myself am only able to "pounce" on an Eileen Fisher dress marked down 50 percent).

Very often, though, you can lead a person to romance but you can't make him drink. You'll have to decide whether staying friends is going to be worth it in the end. Usually it is worth it, because the choice will be between friendship and nothing.

Avoiding the Sound-Bite Social Life

If you live in the modern world, especially an urban area, the following first few minutes of a restaurant rendezvous with a friend might sound familiar:

"Hi Jen! Great to see you! Let's order, shall we? Hold on, I have to take this call ... Hello? Georgie? Oh, it's so great to hear your voice, sweetie, did you get my text? I can't really talk right now, I'm at dinner with someone. Sunday? Great, I can meet you on the west side between 12:30 and 1:15. Okay, bye! Sorry about that, Jen. So, where's that waiter? We have to order, I have to be somewhere by 8:20 ... "

I know someone who, upon a first look, seems to have an enviably full and exciting social life. She has coffee with Joe from 11:45 to 12:20, lunch with Sue from 1:00 to 2:30. She calls to check up with Sally, Moira, and Ted while doing errands. The problem? Quantity, not quality. Busy-ness does not necessarily mean happiness. If this is your social style, you may be living life in the too-fast lane. It's as if your social life is one big channel changer, and your finger is always on the button.

Most of us need to slow down and stay focused on the person in front of us. Why not try a three-hour dinner with someone? You might be surprised at how good it will feel. More dates per day does not equal more love. It is intimacy in friendship—quality relationships—that brings you love.

Let's check in and see how Bob and Joe are doing:

(Ringtone)
BOB: "Hello?"
JOE: "Bobby baby! What about that game last night? Was that sweet, or what!"
BOB: (laughing) "It was indeed."
JOE: "Listen, I've got some ribs with your name on 'em."
BOB: "Ah. I *thought* I left something behind at the game."
(Laughter)
JOE: "Jane and I are having a few people over on Saturday for dinner and we thought you might want to join us. I want to try out my new Weber grill."
BOB: "Wow. Sounds good."
JOE: "Awesome!"

Not everyone you "date" will become your best friend, but one thing is for certain: If you want to deepen your friendships, you must have playdates at each other's homes. Hosting and guesting are the entrées of friendship; everything else has just been the appetizer.

CHAPTER 3

Getting Over Your Hosting Phobia

Eat, Love, Host! Hospitality as a Way of Life

For many of us, having people over is an organic part of our lives;
for others it's right up there with going to the dentist or doing
taxes—it's something that's nerve-wracking, disruptive to daily
life, and to be avoided at all costs. The "non-hosters" invariably
ask, "Why is it so important for me to invite people to my home?
What's the big deal about hosting?"

It's a fair question. Why *should* we roll out the red carpet (and
vacuum it), spend time and money preparing for guests, attend
to their every comfort during their stay, and have to clean up after them once they are gone? What rewards do you reap as host?
If your home is truly your castle, why shouldn't you just keep the
drawbridge up and not let anyone in? Surely if you have worked
hard enough to own a weekend cottage in Cape Cod, it's more desirable, and more efficacious, to go there alone with your mate
(or with your immediate family), so that you can sit around in

your boxers if you want. Not having houseguests is definitely less stressful than having them. And isn't low stress what leisure time is all about?

While some people struggle with feelings of loneliness or disconnectedness and consciously yearn for better friendships, others do not believe anything at all is missing from their lives. Most people have their daily routines—having to do with family life, work life, and recreational pastimes—ultra-organized and will tell you they couldn't fit one more thing into their schedules even if they wanted to.

The trouble is, the same thing can be said of exercise, volunteer work, and other activities that are intrinsic to our nature as well as beneficial to our physical, psychological, and/or spiritual health. If you have never eaten anything in your whole life except porridge, you can't know what you are missing. If you have never traveled outside your own town or city, you don't know how travel can broaden your horizons. Similarly, you can't know what entertaining friends regularly will do for your life until you begin to do it. We all need to find the time for the things that are important.

Several years ago, I ran into a friend of mine who was deep in the doldrums. Her career had stalled, her two small and very demanding kids were completely taking over her life, and she was constantly bickering with her husband. She was behind in everything and couldn't seem to complete even the smallest task. In short, she had the blues—and the blahs. We talked for a while, and I offered her the standard brand of sympathy and advice. Then I went out on a limb.

"What you really need, Katherine, is to give a party," I said with a gleam.

"Oh yeah, *right!* That's just what I need." She laughed as if I had suggested that she wear a pink neon bikini to a PTA meeting. Soon after that, a good friend of mine gave a small dinner and I had the friend invite Katherine. It turned out to be an inspired grouping of guests: two artists, one science academic, two Italian students who were visiting the U.S. on a cycling tour, and Katherine and me. The combination of sensibilities at the table engendered a conversation that was interesting and unusual. Katherine confessed to me later that she had been so depressed that she almost hadn't come to the dinner, but that she was happy she had because her mood was greatly improved for two weeks afterward. Unfortunately, a couple of months later, she started feeling depressed again.

"What you really need, Katherine, is to give a party," I insisted like the broken record I can be. And this time, she did.

It was a modest-sized cocktail party held in her studio, where her six-foot-high abstract paintings stacked against all four walls created an exotic backdrop for the twenty or so guests. Though most of the guests didn't know each other, somehow we started singing bits of old songs and telling outrageously corny jokes. (Yes, of course I was there! You don't think I give this kind of counsel without getting myself invited, do you?) It was an absolutely splendid, invigorating evening. This time, Katherine's spirits were doubly raised; the joy of being in good company was combined with the satisfaction of knowing she had given others a good time.

Obviously, inviting people to your home is a nice thing to do for them. It's actually invitation—not imitation—that is the sincerest form of flattery. It's a gesture of affection, a special gift. You are offering people, for a time, all the comforts of your personal domain. It's the adult version of the sharing we learned (or should have learned) as children.

But here's the real secret: Although hospitality may seem like an act of pure generosity, it is, in fact, a mutually beneficial arrangement. What the guests receive is self-evident, but the host earns praise and gratitude, not to mention (one hopes) return invitations to the guests' houses or events. Having people over is also a way for the host to be reminded of the things that are good in his life, as guests can usually be counted on to ooh and aah over the furniture, the kids, the cats, the new sound system, or the old family portrait hanging in the hallway. In the case of Katherine's party, one of the benefits she received was that her husband saw her in a new light (or rather, an old light he had forgotten)—that of a gracious hostess. Thus she gained the appreciation and admiration of not only her guests but her husband as well.

Katherine told me that the party also helped her to reconnect with friends with whom she felt she was losing contact. One of them is now someone she sees frequently for lunch. This new bond of friendship was forged, in part, because home socializing speeds the friendship process. It says to each guest, "Please be in my life." We all know inviting the potential lover home is an important step, but we forget it is an important step in platonic relationships, too.

I'm not claiming that giving one party solved all of Katherine's problems, or that it will solve yours, but neither would one ten-mile bike ride, one shiatsu massage, or one French class. All of these things can enhance your life if you make a habit of them. So why not make a vow to yourself that every few weeks you are going to have someone over—even if it's only for iced tea and cookies? I promise you'll soon begin to feel the positive effects. In addition, your great get-together will inspire other people to have similar get-togethers. I believe the more we all socialize with each other—especially at home, where the most intimate communication takes place—the better. Being hospitable is ultimately an act of love. Good things come to those who host.

Identifying Your (Un)comfort Zone

Anyone who knows me at all knows I like meeting new people more than I like cheesecake, martinis, and Hugh Grant movies all put together—especially new people who have been hand-picked for me. So when my neighbor Sharon started telling me about a fascinating couple she really wanted me to meet, I was thrilled.

"You will get such a huge kick out of Ronnie and Joe," she said enthusiastically. "You guys have such a lot in common."

I wasn't quite sure what she meant by this, as he was a performance artist and she was a pathologist, but I responded with the appropriate positive noises. Sharon suggested that a dinner party at her house might be the best venue. Immediately my inner social self began to glow happily with anticipation. New people, interesting conversation, and food prepared by someone else—what could be better than that?

And then, all at once, I sensed Sharon faltering in mid-plan. After she had suggested a few possible dates, she started backtracking, saying she wasn't sure if she could "get it together" and that "maybe we'd do it sometime in the future." For me, the eager guest-to-be, it was like having a fish on the line I thought was a sure thing and suddenly feeling it slipping off the hook.

Carefully I tried to ferret out the cause of her hesitation, so I could reel her back in.

"Well, I'd certainly love to meet Ronnie and Joe," I said. "Please don't worry about serving a gourmet meal, if that's what you're thinking. It's just lovely that you want to get us together." Sharon hemmed and hawed and tried to change the subject, but eventually I teased her into confessing her particular brand of hosting phobia. It turned out it wasn't the menu she was worried about.

"It's all the little details. Like...I always worry that someone will go into the guest bathroom and I will have forgotten to put out toilet paper or fresh towels or soap!" She was laughing, but I knew she was serious, too. I also knew this wasn't the real cause of her hesitation.

The reluctance to host exists on several levels. On the surface level are all our mundane excuses: We don't have enough time or money, the house is a wreck, we can't cook well enough, we don't know who to invite. One person told me that he hadn't had a dinner party since the disastrous one he had back in 1997, when two guests got into a political argument and started throwing ice cubes at each other. I tend to worry that the guests will find huge dust bunnies under the table or notice a chip in one of my dishes. I am afraid they will think the art on my walls is not tasteful enough. Mostly I feel anxiety about the fact that, instead of having a party, I should be working or doing something "more constructive." These all sound like reasonable excuses for not hosting, but almost always there are deeper fears beneath the surface.

The first underlying level of hosting phobia is fear of failure. When you host, it is tantamount to taking on a project that is entirely your responsibility. Being the host is an active role, a leadership role; the host is in effect the master of ceremonies. As host, you are volunteering to be in charge of the evening, and therefore you are also in charge of the happiness and comfort of the guests. If the food is bad, you are responsible; when the conversation falters, it is you who must get it back on track. You are the coach of the "team" of guests. Naturally, you may feel that if the team doesn't succeed, it will be your fault. This can make having a party seem like nothing more than an opportunity for disappointment. *What if everyone has a horrible time?* you worry. *What if it's the world's worst party?*

This leads to the next, deepest level of hosting phobia: fear of rejection. It's hard enough for most of us to get up the courage to *go* to a party, so it's no wonder many of us don't want to risk *hosting* one. It's not always easy to recognize this fear in ourselves, but think about it: If we are afraid that everything won't be perfect, what we are really afraid of is that we will be proven to be less than perfect as a person. Deep down, we are afraid that if people see the "real" us, they will not like us anymore. Opening your house means opening yourself—to inspection and to criticism. And it's far safer to stay closed up.

We all have well-crafted images of ourselves that we project to the outside world. Most of us are secretly afraid of someone finding out that we are not who we pretend to be; in fact, studies have shown that 70 percent of us suffer from the imposter syndrome, a feeling that if people were to really know us they would discover we were frauds in some way. Whatever dichotomy there is between who you really are and what you let most people see will be harder to hide when someone visits you in your home. Even if where you live is exquisite and spotless, it's still extremely personal and therefore revealing. Whether your house is crammed with family memorabilia, painted bubblegum pink, or appointed with your ex-husband's black leather furniture, having people see you in it can be unsettling.

Even during the preliminary act of the invitation process— during which potential guests will, of course, answer yes or no—we have to face our insecurities. Who will and won't come to the party we give? Who do we even want to come? Having a party can force us to take stock of who we know, who we wish we knew—and who we wish knew us. Every time you give a party, it's an assessment of your social life: Shouldn't you have more friends by now? Are these friends really indicative of who you are? Will they hate each other?

What if you give a party and no one comes? (Of course, if you have *really* low self-esteem, you may feel that anyone who would actually come to a party hosted by you is not someone you really want to hang out with. If this is true for you, close this book right now and go get some psychotherapy. And thank you so much for coming.)

The cure for hosting phobia is relatively simple. It's in the doing. You can start off with having people over for bagels and coffee if you want, but you must start hosting on a regular basis. If you keep in mind these five basic laws of hosting, it will help:

The Five Laws of Hosting

1. Everyone is already grateful to you as soon as they walk in the door.
2. Everyone has been a host, and is therefore empathetic.
3. It's the guests' responsibility as well as the host's to help make the event a success.
4. No one is thinking about you; they are thinking about themselves.
5. Have a good time and your guests will, too.

You're Not Martha Stewart: How to Take the Pressure Off

Everyone knows someone who is a "perfect host" or hostess. The perfect hostess gives fabulous, elegant dinner parties about once a month. These are dinner parties that the blessedly invited talk about for years—dinner parties that poets write poems about and painters paint paintings about. The perfect host starts planning the menu a week ahead, shops three days in advance, and starts cooking at least one day before—rolling seaweed for sushi, baking pie crust for the key lime pie, making homemade sorbet. When the guests arrive, there are fresh candles (she dips them herself), fresh linens, fresh lilies floating in a bowl in the loo. No microscopic spec of dust exists on any surface to offend the senses of her awed guests. Not one morsel of food served is less than a culinary masterpiece.

We worship the perfect hostess and perfect host; they are the Goddess and God of the dinner party. Unfortunately, they are also a big part of the hosting problem. Though we all aspire to the ideal state of hostliness they embody, we know without question we are bound to fall short of this ideal. The result? Nine out of ten of us mere mortals chicken out (or go out and order chicken) when faced with the idea of being the host.

Don't let the perfect hostess experiences you have had, read about, or seen in movies intimidate you. Don't worry. It's actually an act of kindness to others to be less than perfect. It makes everyone feel better about themselves! You will be forgiven for anything and everything except rudeness or bodily injury. Just keep in mind the fifth law of hosting: Have a good time and your guests will, too.

Whether you decide to have people over for pizza and a game of Uno at your kitchen table, or you decide to have weekend guests at your exclusive country compound, here are a few simple strategies to help you to remember you do not have to be Martha Stewart, Rachael Ray, or the Duchess of Windsor.

Be a Good Lister

I have known of hosts who, on the day of the party, will stand frozen in the middle of their living room chewing their fingernails and muttering to themselves, "What do I do first, what do I do first?" While some people have fantastic, photographic memories for details, it's absolutely essential for most of us regular humans to make a list. Not just any list, but a numbered list, in order of priority. It is surprising how many of us start with the least important thing (often the easiest, most fun thing)—such as arranging the flowers—when there are dirty socks splayed across the piano keys and not a morsel of food in the house.

The top of your list should have only the few vitally important items, which you should do before anything else. For example:

1. Invite people
2. Buy food
3. Clear off dining room table/move laundry off piano
4. Make sure there is enough booze
5. Get dressed (I often forget this last one)

Everything else—making salad dressing, scrubbing the tub, vacuuming—is extra credit! What's the worst that can happen? You make the salad dressing while the guests are there, close the shower curtain, and keep the lights down low.

Cooking Without Ego (That's "Ego," Not "Egg")

At the risk of insulting some readers, I must tell you that I am of the opinion that failing to have a dinner party because you think you can't cook well enough is often not an issue of insecurity but one of narcissism. When you have people over, your emphasis should be on them, not on you. Your first duty is to give your guests a good time, not to display your skills. In other words, unless you serve them burnt carrots and raw pork, your cooking prowess is of secondary importance. Of course, if you cook a gourmet meal because you truly love to do it and you want to please your guests, that's fine, but I think many people these days see cooking as a status symbol, like driving a Porsche or having the biggest house on the block.

Obviously, delicious and interesting food enhances a dinner party, but it is decidedly *not* more important than good conversation, the welcoming attitude of the host, or the comfort of the home in general. So have fun making something you will love to eat, even try something tricky if you want, but do not let the idea of culinary excellence interfere with your impulse to invite people into your home.

You are not required to cook for your guests at all if you don't want to. There are many other options for entertaining. But here are some tension-reducing tips to help you relax when you are cooking for guests:

REPEAT PERFORMANCE: If you already know how to make boeuf bourguignon so well you could do it in your sleep, by all means make it. Make it often. Make it for every dinner party you have. Just be sure to keep track of what guests you invite to these particular meals. You don't want to serve the same people the same thing over and over. (You should never let guests know their meal is a rerun.)

ONE-DISH WONDER: If the idea of preparing a five-course meal and having it all ready at exactly 8:35 frightens you (as well it should), narrow your focus. Make just one impressive dish and let the rest take care of itself. It's okay if the dish is hard to make, because you aren't going to have to worry about anything else. The rest of the meal can consist of simple-to-cook items (baked potatoes, steamed vegetables), or can be store bought and ready-to-serve. If your one dish comes out well, that's all that matters.

KITCHEN LIFELINES: Have a backup team. Although I have been known to make some truly memorable meals, I am not a gourmet cook. However, I have several friends who *are* gourmet cooks, and I have them all on speed dial. That way, when, an hour before the guests come I suddenly panic and can't remember whether I am supposed to leave the lid on or off the pot roast, I can check with someone easily without wasting a lot of time and without getting frazzled thumbing through cookbooks. These gourmet friends are also very useful for pre–dinner party therapy. They tell me not to worry that I bought dried figs instead of fresh and that I'm crazy to think anyone is going to care if the wine glasses don't all match because one of my neighbors broke one earlier that day. Note: Be sure these "spotters" are not going to be insulted if they are not invited to your party. Mine are, for the most part, out-of-town friends.

"The Maid Who Never Came" and Other Face-Saving Excuses

Now, take a really deep breath. You're having people over tonight and you're feeling low energy. Therefore you are about to do something really radical. Get ready, get set—and *don't* clean the house. Really, I mean it. Don't scrub the floors, don't polish the furniture, don't dust the lamps. Okay, you can pick your wife's bike pants and helmet up off the floor, move stuff that's in the doorway which guests can trip on, and deal with the dirty dishes on top of the TV, but that's all. Never forget that almost no one has a spotless, ordered household in their day-to-day life. It's not just you!

Actually, not cleaning up at all is virtually impossible for anyone over eighteen, and most of the time I can't do it myself. And I should mention that if you are expecting special guests (your boss, your mother-in-law, the Secretary of State), it is probably not all that good an idea to have an untidy house. But once in a while, not straightening up can remind you that having people over isn't necessarily a big deal, and you could do it more often.

So try it, especially when the guests are people who already know you and have seen your house. (Wait! I see you...Put that Swiffer down. No one cares about the crumbs under the stove.)

If your place *is* in a state of disarray when the guests arrive, usually the best course of action is not to draw any attention to it, for it is a surprising truth that often what seems an unsightly, god-awful mess to you will not even be noticed by other people. But sometimes it will make you feel more comfortable (and it can be a nice icebreaker) to offer one of the following explanations to your guests upon their arrival:

• "I'm so embarrassed! You'll have to forgive the state of the house; the maid never came."

• "I am terribly sorry for the mess in here. I started to clean up and pulled a muscle in my back (arm, leg, foot, etc.)."

• "I can't believe you are seeing the house this way—I was just about to straighten up and I got an emergency call from a neighbor...You can blame the Stellmans for the mess."

• "Pardon all the clutter, but I've (we've) been on deadline for work and it's just been insane around here."

• "I was so glad it was *you* coming to dinner—I feel so comfortable with you I didn't feel like I had to make everything spic and span."

The Value of Spontaneity

On the other hand, if you invite people at the very last minute, you can't possibly be expected to have cleaned much, right? The spur-of-the-moment gathering is one of the best ways to trick yourself out of your hosting phobia. Like the skydiver who forces himself not to think about it until it's time to jump out of the plane, you can avoid many of your party fears if you have less time to worry about it. The closer your invitation is to the date of the event, the lower the expectations of your guests. More important, there's no time to worry, no time to clean, no time to make a gourmet meal! Impromptu get-togethers also make you look like one of those carefree, super-cool people we all wanted to be when we grew up. ("Why don't you come over? I just threw a leg of lamb in the oven.")

Hosting for Dummies: Almost Effortless Entertaining

When you mention entertaining friends, many people conjure up a picture of a long table with a white tablecloth, gleaming silver candlesticks, sterling flatware, crystal bowls, and well-dressed guests sitting straight up in their chairs helping themselves to a multitude of steaming dishes. (Okay, maybe this is just me. Maybe you think of a round table with no tablecloth and people using chopsticks.)

Dear reader, repeat after me: *There is no need to have a dinner party.* There are countless other ways to entertain your friends and acquaintances than having a dinner party. Dinner parties can be daunting if you are not used to giving them (although I will show you later how they don't have to be). And there are a lot of other much easier ways to entertain people than cooking them an entire formal meal.

Coffee, Tea, and Me

Inviting someone for coffee or tea is completely painless, and yet so very intimate. Think Mary Tyler Moore in the old *Dick Van Dyke Show* (if you are old enough to know what that is). It's neighborly, it's super-casual. The wonderful thing about having someone over for coffee or tea is that there is no sense of social commitment or obligation, because you have not put yourself out at all. Your guest (or guests) won't feel she must reciprocate. It's no pressure, no stress. It's also perfect for when you want to send a more casual signal to someone than the one a dinner invitation might send. Inviting someone over for a drink or for coffee can be a good "let's see how it is to have this person in my house before I put him on my regular guest list" move. The great thing is, it is something we do with our best friends as well as our acquaintances. In my opinion, we do not have people over for coffee enough these days. (I blame Starbucks.)

The Beauty of Having Them in for Drinks

Don't tell anyone, but drink dates are often thinly disguised dinner dates.

I am often invited over to friends' homes for "a drink." What invariably happens is that, first of all, it's not "a drink" but several drinks and, second, somehow there is always food. Sometimes it is a makeshift dinner with the hostess and her kids around the kitchen table and sometimes it's a hefty supply of hors d'oeuvres with eight other guests. Either way, it feels just like dinner to the stomach. For the host, having friends in for drinks removes the pressure of having to cook. If they are invited just for a drink, then everything else you serve will feel like a bonus and will be appreciated that much more. On the other hand, if there isn't any food, they can't complain, because after all it was just a "drinks" date. This can be a totally liberating thing of beauty for the host.

Note: You do have to serve at least a little something to nibble on with drinks, even if it's just peanuts.

No-Shame Takeout

Several people I interviewed have recounted perfectly wonderful evenings of having friends over and ordering takeout instead of cooking. Whether it's Vietnamese food or Kentucky Fried Chicken, the most important thing about having people over for takeout is that you eat it off of real china, not paper plates, and that you sit around a table. The takeout dinner party is more prevalent, of course, in urban areas, where every imaginable kind of food can be delivered to your door. In non-urban areas we're talking basically pizza, which is really only appropriate to serve when eating is a secondary part of the gathering (such as during a poker party).

When having people in for takeout, the proper procedure is to consult with your guests on what to order. That is part of the fun of takeout. No matter what you decide to order (as a group), you can share everything. The sharing of food is a key element of the whole experience. Naturally, you must let people know before they come that you are ordering in.

Note: In most cases, the host pays, unless it is a last-minute arrangement and the guests are good friends (for example, when you are all going to the theater and eating takeout is simply easier than going to a restaurant).

Nightcapping

Another marvelous compromise between cooking dinner for people and going to a restaurant is to plan to have everyone back to your house after the restaurant for a "nightcap" or for dessert and coffee. For people who have tiny apartments, no dining room table, or no desire to cook, this is a perfect half-hosting position. You still get the intimacy of having people over, and since you have just eaten with them at the restaurant, your conversation is already primed—ready for that end-of-the-night bonding.

Open House, Insert Guests

I often think this is the very best of the dinner party alternatives. It is, in many ways, the most worry-free kind of party. The invitation to an "open house" usually specifies a rather long time period (for example, 2:00 to 8:00) during which guests are expected to "drop by." They can come for a half hour or stay for six. Allowing the guests to come and go as they please creates a fluid atmosphere that is relaxing to both the guests and the host. The open house also necessitates that the host serve food that he has already prepared, bought ready-made, or had catered; the bar can even be self-serve. This cuts the duties of the host way down during the party, so that he can focus on talking to the guests (and having fun!).

There are many occasions that warrant having an open house: a housewarming, a shower, a national holiday, the arrival of something new in your house—like a new baby or a new baby grand. Or you can have an open house just because you like to entertain in this particular style. For years, a colleague of mine hosted what he called "Second Tuesdays," inspired by the Victorian practice of being "at home." Every second Tuesday of the month, he had people over to his apartment. In the beginning, he had to call everyone and remind them, but after a while people started remembering on their own. He would invite many different kinds of people—some he had known for years and others he had met only once at a party. Some Tuesdays, only two people would show up and they would have an intimate conversation about their childhoods or their sex lives, and other times twenty-five people would come, making it more of a cocktail party. My colleague encouraged those who came to bring food and drink, but he did it in a very low-pressure way. ("There will be stuff to eat and drink, but bringing something would be wonderful, only if you have time. But bring yourself for sure.")

Having an open house is a very generous thing for you, as host, to do. You are committing to five or six hours of entertaining, and yet ask no real commitment of time from your guests. You also must be prepared to spend a lot of time saying hello and good-bye to people.

There are some people who don't just hold an "open house" event, but who truly have an *open house*. I interviewed one man, a fairly famous actor, who surprised me by telling me that, contrary to what I would imagine for someone in his profession, he and his wife (and their five children) had a perennially open house. Their friends all knew they could come over at any time. There was usually a pot of chili or bouillabaisse on the stove. How this man manages his marriage, his privacy, and his sanity is beyond me, but he is one of the happiest and nicest people I have ever met.

B.Y.O.E. (Bring Your Own Everything)

This leads me to the most effortless (and most un-chic) kind of party. The B.Y.O.E. (Bring Your Own Everything) party. Cheesy? Maybe. But easy? Oh, baby! I know Emily Post would probably not approve, as it is really like cheating at the game of hosting, but there are some instances when you can get away with it.

I got into the habit of doing this years ago when I had no money and still wanted to have parties. One day in early March, I was feeling as if I needed to put a little zing back into my life, so I called up thirty or forty people I knew and said to them, "I'm having an 'Ides of March' party. I'm providing the people, the music, and the sofa and chairs. Bring everything else." It was a gutsy thing to do, and many of my friends teased me about it. But they knew I was broke, and I happened to have a large apartment that was really great for parties. And, P.S., everyone had a marvelous time.

You do have to spell it out carefully when you have a B.Y.O.E. party. "I'm having people over to watch *Desperate Housewives*. Bring whatever you want to drink and eat for yourself. And bring a desperate housewife if you know one!" Or "I'm having a bunch of people in on Saturday. I've got a case of beer and six bottles of red wine. Everyone has to bring everything else. Bring food—I'm hungry!"

I'll admit that unless you are a starving artist, you can't really tell people to B.Y.O.E. more than once or twice in your hosting lifetime. You can, of course, always have people bring wine or beer, or dessert. And, while B.Y.O.E. is certainly the cheapest way to go, you may find it's not all that costly or difficult to have a good old-fashioned cocktail party.

The Pros and Cons of the Cocktail Party

Cocktail parties have been around since the early twentieth century. Dozens of famous people have had nothing but bad things to say about them: Comedian Fred Allen once said, "A cocktail party is a gathering held to enable forty people to talk about themselves at the same time. The man who remains after the liquor is gone is the host." Equally disdainful, socialite Elsa Maxwell called the cocktail party "easily the worst invention since castor oil." Nevertheless, the cocktail party remains alluring—perhaps because we can't forget the vision of Bette Davis on the stairs with her martini in *All About Eve*, or Audrey Hepburn and that long cigarette holder in *Breakfast at Tiffany's*. And though there may be a decided lack of intimacy about these affairs, I must confess I love them. They can be exciting and high energy. They provide a safe place to talk to strangers while drinking, and there are usually too many people there to ever be bored. The cocktail party is nothing less than a human tasting menu. (And you can quote me on that.) Let's look at the pros and cons of having a cocktail party:

PROS

1. I hate to state the obvious, but one of the main pros of a cocktail party is, er, well, the cocktails! It may not seem like the most healthy or politically correct notion, but a little alcohol can enhance social situations. Cocktails are a social lubricant; they help people to relax and have a good time. It's almost guaranteed.

2. It's great for inviting new acquaintances—people who you don't quite know well enough yet to invite to dinner. It's not a major time commitment for them and it's a good showcase for you—they can see who your other friends are.

3. A cocktail party also allows you to return invitations. In one fell swoop you can pay everybody back who's invited you to anything over the past six months.

4. Since cocktail parties are often large, you can mix together a lot of people you couldn't at a dinner party. That rather stuffy Republican investment banker you know and your friend who started a lefty commune in Vermont will be buffered by everyone else. At a dinner party, they might find themselves uncomfortable sitting next to each other.

5. A cocktail party can be glamorous and impressive. There is a kind of "no holds barred" feeling about it, and it shows a willingness to reveal all the social corners of your life. It's exciting for the guests, who never know who they are going to meet. A

cocktail party says, "I love many people and I want them all to know each other."

6. It's fun for you, the host! You will know all (or almost all) of the people there. It is life-affirming to put all of the people you know in your house, all together. It's a mini-celebration of your life. The pure energy of it is intoxicating, never mind the daiquiris.

Cons

1. Cocktail parties tend to be superficial affairs. You, as the host, will have no meaningful conversations with anyone. Period. So don't expect to. There is a famous anecdote about the editor Maxwell Perkins: Arriving at a cocktail party one evening in an endeavor to test the hypothesis that no one listens to what anyone says on such occasions, he greeted his hostess with a polite handshake and the following words: "Sorry I'm late, but it took me longer to strangle my aunt than I expected." "Yes, indeed," his hostess replied. "I'm so happy you came."

2. Cocktail parties can be too brief. The minute they get started, they are over. If you have a cocktail party from 6:00 to 8:00, or even 5:30 to 8:00, people will come and stay for a half hour on their way somewhere else. So unless you have help, you are basically saying hello and good-bye all evening. It's a lot of work for such a very short, loud affair.

3. It can be a free-for-all. Depending on your crowd, something happens to people drinking in a large group. They are likely to put their wet glasses on your piano and their shrimp tails on your night table. And when it comes to cocktail parties, people think nothing of failing to R.S.V.P. or bringing a person (or five) without any notice; you never know exactly who is going to show up.

4. You need to invite a lot of people for it to be successful. This depends on the size of your home, of course. I used to live in a teeny-tiny apartment in Little Italy and if I had a cocktail party for fifteen people it felt like a hundred. Why must you have a crowd? Because to get people to mingle, they must be standing up; and to keep them standing, there must be no room for sitting. To attain the necessary critical mass, you may have to invite people you wouldn't really socialize with ordinarily—or people you hardly know.

5. Cocktail parties can be costly, and if you don't have a partner and you can't afford help, it is a lot of work. In past eras, as long as you had plenty of liquor and some cheese and crackers, you were good to go; but now, with many people not drinking and so many "foodies" around, you really must make an effort with the food.

Look! It seems as though the pros outweigh the cons. Your cocktail party can range from casual (serve-yourself) to elegant (waiters passing food and a professional bartender). You don't have to make all the snacks yourself. If you provide the cocktails, it's perfectly acceptable to have people bring hors d'oeuvres.

Theme Parties and Other Diversionary Tactics

Theme parties may seem like adventurous undertakings, but besides being wonderful fun, the themes act as smokescreens to take the focus off of you, your house, your china, your cooking, or whatever other silly thing you are worried about. You and your hosting skills become secondary to the theme. The theme party is really a gimmick, a con artist trick to guarantee enjoyment.

Theme parties—especially ones that encourage people to express themselves in a creative way—can be memorably, exceptionally convivial. They can be as traditional as a tree trimming, or as bold and wacky as a "red party," where everyone comes dressed in red and all the food is red, too. (Or even a blue party: Alfred Hitchcock, a legendary practical joker, was said to have held "blue dye" dinner parties at which guests were served blue martinis, blue steaks, and blue potatoes.)

TV Parties

I admit that I have an extreme point of view about television and socializing. I believe that television is a powerful drug, and that turning on a TV in a room full of people is a little bit like handing around syringes filled with heroin. I also believe it is a crutch we really should be learning to socialize without. (Although it may not be possible for two straight guys to ever get together at home without turning on a game.)

Nevertheless, there are certain occasions when it makes an enjoyable and almost obligatory party: The Superbowl, the night of a presidential election, or, if you absolutely must, one of the trendy shows people love to watch together (*True Blood, Desperate Housewives, Project Runway*). Serve something that is easy to eat while sitting on the floor or juggling a plate on the lap, and make sure everyone knows that television is going to be the main event. If at all possible, turn off the TV before and after the show and talk to each other (instead of shouting at the screen).

Costume Party and Its Variants

Full-on costume parties can be hard to pull off, unless it is Halloween, but they are worth it if you can get people into the spirit. Putting on a costume releases some latent wild spirit in us all.

If you think your guests will resist a costume party (by that I mean they will not come at all), try just having a "hat party" or a "funny tie" night—something that doesn't require too much on the part of the guests and ensures a good spirit at the party.

Here are a few ideas for festive fun:

· Black Tie (or creative black tie—which means people can come in tuxedos and sneakers)
· Retro Dress-Up ('60s, '70s, '80s)
· Tropical Island (i.e., Hawaiian shirts)
· Come Dressed as You Were on the Happiest Day of Your Life
· Come Dressed as the Host
· Come Dressed as Your Favorite Writer (painter, celebrity, etc.)

Are You Game?

There are hundreds—probably thousands—of books written for hosts and hostesses, mostly dating from the 1920s, '30s, and '40s, and in all of them you will find the bulk of the book is on games. Games are relaxing and divert the participants from their day-to-day lives; also, playing games offers people a structure within which to learn about each other. (It's the way we got to know each other as children—by playing together, not by talking about the weather.) Most games stretch brain muscles, and the prospect of winning or losing adds excitement to the evening. The best games to play at a party are ones during which you can gain knowledge or increase a skill by playing. It's best not to play card games—bridge, hearts, poker—unless all the guests are already good friends, as card games tend to inhibit socializing during play.

Be certain everyone present wants to play the proposed game. If a guest does not want to play, drop the whole idea. One unhappy or uncomfortable guest equals an unsuccessful party.

A Word About Word Games

Word games, such as Scrabble, Fictionary, Boggle, Outburst, etc., are great intellectual sport, but they are also dangerous. A friend you never suspected of having even the slightest competitive streak can be suddenly screaming at the top of her lungs that a particular word is certainly in *her* dictionary, and what kind of idiotic dictionary does the hostess have anyway?

The White Elephant and Other Gift Swaps

For a "white elephant" party, each of the guests brings a wrapped gift—something from home he wants to get rid of—and places it in a pile. (Sometimes it's a store-bought gift, in which case it is usually valued under $10.) Whoever goes first (you can pick numbers from a hat) unwraps a gift from the pile. Each successive guest can either 1) "steal" an already opened gift or 2) go for a wrapped gift from the pile. The best thing about a white elephant party is that this particular kind of gift exchange is often funny while at the same time revealing something personal about the guests. (Eventually it is usually divulged, by means of jokes and teasing, what each guest brought and where it came from.) By the end of the party, you will know interesting tidbits about the lives and tastes of other guests—things that you would, in all likelihood, never have found out at a dinner or cocktail party. It's almost as if the participants are sharing the contents of their closets (the way we did as children). It's also interesting to see which gifts people go for. Just who is vying for the black apron with the martini glasses on it? Who seems eager for the Bob Dylan CD? Who wants the plastic inflatable Austin Powers chair?

A more simple version of this is for everyone to bring a gift and take one from the pile, with no further exchanges. This is a perfect opportunity for re-gifting, though you'd better make certain the original gift-giver isn't at the party! Or you can add to a January invitation, "Bring the worst present you received for Christmas," and swap them around. I like to call this party "Aunt Franny's Fruitcake Party."

The Classics
Many people like to "go retro" and play one of the classics: charades, twenty questions, Mad Libs, or Monopoly, just to name a few games. This can be fun if everyone is in the right, fairly silly frame of mind. I myself refuse to play charades after a horrible experience I once had in Chicago. I was stuck in a remote suburb with no way home and everyone in the house was playing an endless game of charades—not just charades, but sailing charades (!), where all the answers were words like "wind" or "anchor." I'm afraid I was scarred for life.

Doing Dinner:
From Potluck to Posh

While there are plenty of ways to invite people into your home, dinner parties are the ultimate. Eating together is something humans have done together since the beginning of time. (Animals eat alone; people shouldn't.) This is one of the reasons people who live by themselves end up turning on the TV; they need other people to share the experience of eating, and when they can't get real people, they have to settle for facsimiles. As Epicurus said, "We should look for someone to eat and drink with before looking for something to eat and drink; for dining alone is leading the life of a lion or wolf." For me, dinner parties are magical; good things will often result. (If you don't believe me, just ask the founders of YouTube. That billion-dollar idea came out of a conversation at a dinner party among friends.)

When you decide to invite people over for dinner, it might help to focus on this idea of sharing rather than on the idea of wow-ing your guests. Don't think, *I am throwing a dinner party.* Think instead, *I am going to have people over.* Remember, there is no such thing as a disastrous dinner party, unless you actually stab one of the guests or they all get violently ill. The food can be burned, the electricity can go out, the dog can pee in people's shoes and still the guests are likely to call the next day and say, "Wonderful dinner party. Thanks so much for having me!" And they will mean it.

Two's Company

Inviting just one person over is a great way to start. It's really no harder than cooking for yourself, and you can either prepare the food while you and your guest have a drink or cook together. I often give my guest a small chore that is easily done while we're both in the kitchen together. Dinner for two promotes the sharing of confidences with the food. It usually makes for a very relaxed evening, and by the end you will feel like much better friends.

Potluck

This is a wonderful option if you are suffering from either lack of confidence or lack of funds. Still very socially acceptable, this is a gathering of people where each person is expected to bring a dish of food to be shared among the group. The term "potluck" is mis-leadingly negative; I have always felt these meals should be called "team dinners" or "socialized suppers." This kind of event is the perfect thing to organize when you feel that cooking an entire meal by yourself for ten people is completely impossible. Believe me, it's still work to get the house ready, have the right serving plates and glasses, and coordinate a tasty meal. But because of the communal experience of eating (and the sense of intimacy that can ensue), nothing beats the pitching-in feeling of a potluck.

Note: Remember to have your guests take their pots and platters with them when they leave.

Pseudo Potluck

Many people are more familiar with this incarnation of the potluck. It's a benign "bait and switch" version of entertaining.

First, you invite a number of people to a dinner party at your home. The guests accept your invitation. As the date for the party nears—perhaps even the morning of the party—the guests invariably ask, "What can I bring?" At which point you say, "Well, actually, so-and-so is bringing the pâté, and so-and-so is bringing the salad. Would you mind terribly bringing the dessert?" And somehow, even though you have invited people over to dinner, you end up only having to roast the lamb. Yet, because you have arranged the gathering and have prepared the main course, it still feels like you produced the whole dinner.

Note: Do be sure, though, to compliment each of the guests on their contribution. And do so in front of the other guests.

Picnics

Picnics do not really count as in-home entertaining. But if your living room ceiling suddenly caves in and the weather looks good, pack up the food and have a picnic. It's certainly more intimate than (and therefore preferable to) relocating to a restaurant. The pluses: fresh air, fresh air, and fresh air. The drawbacks: no bathrooms, the possibility of bugs, and the likelihood that someone will spill wine on your blanket.

Traditional Dinner Party

The best sit-down dinners are for six to ten people. Guests may offer to bring wine, but do not ask them to bring anything else. In fact, it is really only appropriate in the case of a traditional dinner party to bring flowers or wine. Anything else may be considered insulting; the idea is that the hostess has already planned everything to go together perfectly.

Tip: Unless you have a kitchen that is connected to your living room area (allowing you to talk to your guests while you cook), organize the menu so that you can prepare most of the food in advance. The less you have to do while your guests are there, the more fun you will have.

Posh

The posh dinner party usually has more than three courses and a different wine for every course. Everything is super-gourmet and expensive. Usually there are eight or more guests. The only way to host a truly successful posh dinner party if you have hosting phobia is to be rich enough to hire help. Otherwise, you may be able to throw one posh dinner party a year if you plan everything months in advance. But I don't recommend it. I say pish-tosh to posh! Leave it to the very rich and enjoy it if you get invited. In any case, posh dinners are not usually the ones where you remember what a good time you had; you only remember the paintings, the china, the caviar, and the butler.

By this time you should be sufficiently over your hosting reticence (or at least well on your way), and chomping at the bit to have people over. Now for the nitty-gritty—the techniques of being a host.

CHAPTER 4

How to Host with the Most

What is it about some parties that makes you feel lucky to be included, reluctant to leave, and hoping to get invited back again? It's not the furniture, the food, or even the other guests as much as it is the host. But what, exactly, constitutes good hosting? Do we have to be born with a flair for entertaining, or is it something we can all learn?

Being an accomplished cook and having a comfortable home certainly helps, but the success of a host is mostly dependent on how he interacts with his guests. It's the ability to put people at ease, make them feel wanted, and know what to do when things don't go as planned that are the hallmarks of a great host. Of paramount importance is the ability to make each and every guest feel welcome.

The Welcome Mat

The word "welcome" comes from the old English *wilcuma*, meaning "one whose coming is pleasing." To make someone feel welcome is to make him feel that you are truly pleased to see him—not just because you invited him and he has shown up more or less on time, but because he is who he is. A good host makes each guest feel wanted; a great host makes each guest feel special, as if it is this *particular* person, of all the people in the world who could be standing at his door, whom the host has most longed to see. This doesn't mean you have to be insincere. It just means being loving, enthusiastic, and in the moment. You *are* happy to see the guest, are you not? You just have to show it. Trust me, no one is so confident, so deeply secure, that he doesn't love to hear, "Michael! So good to see you, man! I am so glad you're here!"

There is a reason the word "welcome" is printed on mats outside the front door. Even if we are not conscious of it, we all experience some anxiety when we are about to cross another's threshold; the welcome mat says to visitors, "Don't be nervous. We will be happy to see you!" Deep down, we still harbor a primal, animal fear associated with entering someone else's territory. This is why it is vital to make guests feel that you are truly glad they are there, and that while they are under your roof, all of their needs are going to be met. It's not always easy to convey all this while you are juggling coats and hats and making sure the dog doesn't run out the open door, but the first few minutes a guest is in your home are very important.

Take the guest's coat and hat (and any bundles she seems disposed to relinquish), making sure she knows where it is you are putting everything. Offer the guest a drink. Introduce her to anyone else present, including any children and pets. Give your guest some idea as to where she might sit down. If she has never

If she has never been to your house before, make sure she knows where the bathroom is.

Now, even though you are going to attempt to cater to all your guests' desires, it is also essential that you remain subtly in control. Your guests need to feel taken care of, but they need to feel that you are doing it with a firm hand. In this way, being a host is like being a parent. The first thing you need to control? The guest list.

The People Recipe: How to Creatively Combine People with Delicious Results

As important as the food menu—or more important—is the human menu. This is not really an issue if you are having an enormous cocktail party where you have invited everyone you know and have encouraged them to bring others. But for smaller gatherings, mixing the right people together requires some thought—or good instinct. You must think about it the same way you would food: How will certain combinations go together? How can I get the best balance at the table? Inviting your old fraternity buddy together with your wife's Reiki guru may be as unpalatable to the assemblage as serving turkey gravy on ice cream.

Of course, you can always invite the same old gang, people who have been friends for years and who you know will get along. But a good host must be generous and adventurous enough to—at least occasionally—put people together who don't know each other well (or at all) and who might find each other interesting. These are often the parties that enrich people's lives. It should give you pleasure to introduce people to each other; helping people connect is an act of social enlightenment.

Getting a good mix is not just a matter of putting people who are similar together. In fact, sometimes the right combination of wildly mismatched individuals can produce a sort of social miracle. I once went with great trepidation to a four-person dinner that included two guests who had been known to fight with each other like hungry wolves over everything—politics, movies, the weather, the seating arrangement. To my intense relief, the fourth guest was so zany and so different from everyone else that it completely changed the interpersonal chemistry. It turned out to be a rollicking, if somewhat bizarre, evening.

I do not advise, however, that you simply spin your Rolodex and select random guests for your party just because you think they might be available or because you owe them an invite. This is like shutting your eyes at the grocery store, grabbing things off the shelves blind, and hoping that everything you end up with will go together.

One person I interviewed told me about a dinner party that smacked of this haphazard approach. Besides this person and her escort (both forty-ish tenants'-rights lawyers), the guests included three nineteen-year-old boys in T-shirts from Germany who spoke no English, a woman whose husband didn't show (but his place card was there anyway), and a supercilious seventy-five-year-old dowager, Mrs. Dobson, who was clearly used to hobnobbing with only the upper upper-crust. The well-intentioned hostess put the Germans near her, as she herself spoke German, but that left the other end of the table cut off from the host and the Germans, dealing with the imposing Mrs. Dobson. The food itself was exquisite, but the conversation was stop and go.

You won't want to use the "opposites attract" theory when arranging a social gathering. Combining people who have extremely different views about politics or religion is not a good idea. Although it can be interesting and refreshing to invite guests who have different lifestyles, if there is also a language barrier or a major age difference at the table, it can be too much. Ex-romantic partners may also not be the best choice for your dinner party unless you are *sure* they have become good friends, and even then you have to be careful that the new mates are both okay with it.

I know some master hosts who keep a "dinner book" to help remember who does and doesn't go well together, along with what was served and so on. However, I don't think I could ever forget my own guest list mistakes. And I am sorry to tell you that some of these are inevitable if you host regularly.

Don't overanalyze the guest list; just close your eyes and imagine for a moment the people you are considering having together in your home. Imagine what they will say to one another. Then trust your hostly instincts.

The Invitation Waltz

Let's assume you have been brilliant in the people-mixing department, and have selected the perfect guests for your dinner party. Now all you have to do is get them there.

The process of picking a date and getting the invitees to commit to coming on that date can be like trying to build a house of cards during a tornado. In fact, the process can be so stressful that many people don't host simply because they don't have the time and energy for the invitation *meshugaas*. I've seen other people begin and then just give up and cancel the whole affair. E-mail does make it a lot easier, and it certainly is acceptable to use e-mail for everything except weddings and formal affairs. But that can have its own problems.

My friend Victoria decided one May that she would host a dinner party, partly because she wanted to introduce Friend A to Friend B. She also owed a dinner to Friends C, D, and E, all of whom she believed would make lively additions to the party. She began by calling person A. Person A said she couldn't come on the 20th but was free on the 21st. Person B was then called. Alas, she wasn't free on the 20th or the 21st, but mightn't the dinner be scheduled for the next weekend? She *so* wanted to meet Friend A. In the meantime, Victoria had e-mailed Friends C, D, and E and asked them if they could come to dinner on the 21st. One said he could make the 21st, and the other said the only day she was free the whole month was the 20th. The last person never answered. Invitational chaos. Victoria had to go back to the drawing board.

A well-executed invitation process is like a waltz, in that there are three steps.

STEP 1: Pin down the main guests while never letting the secondary guests know they are secondary. (By "secondary" I do not mean anything derogatory, merely that for this particular event, these are not the guests who are the main focus.)

STEP 2: Set the date only after the "primary" guests are secured.

STEP 3: Invite the secondary guests, perhaps e-mailing both the primary and secondary guests together with an "official" invitation to dinner on such-and-such a date. If you are lucky, the secondary guests never have to know that you called to invite the primary guests first.

Note: If you have invited people to a dinner far in advance, always call or e-mail a day or two before to remind them.

This system is not only for dinner parties. If you are having a large party—a cocktail, housewarming, birthday, or holiday party—it is not a bad idea to call up ten or so of your most desired guests and take an unofficial poll ("Are you available on the 16th of next month? I may be having a bash"). Then set the date and send a group e-mail invitation out.

As a rule, only three fourths of your invitees are likely to show up at your cocktail party or any other large shindig. There are always some people who will bail out on these parties at the last minute, so you can't even trust the R.S.V.P. number. If you want fifty people, you must invite at least seventy-five. When you invite that many people, it is considered bad form to reveal all the e-mail addresses, so in general you should use the BCC function of your e-mail for your invitation. However, there are select occasions where it is advantageous to let small groups within the large group know they are all invited. I had a big party last year and invited college friends; I made sure I sent them a separate e-mail invitation with the addresses revealed. Not only did it motivate them all to come, but many were grateful to obtain each other's e-mail addresses.

Recovering from Invitational Faux Pas

Most people will feel bad about being left out of an event. Try to never talk about the details of social events in front of someone who you haven't invited or are not going to invite. This is one of the most common ways in which people can be hurt in socializing and in friendship. It is possible that the non-invited person won't be hurt, but you should never take this chance. Discretion is the better part of kindness.

Obviously you can't always invite everyone to everything. If you do accidentally hurt someone's feelings in this way, the best thing to do is to downplay the event ("Oh, that dinner was so ridiculous/

boring/no big deal; no one laughed the whole night") and make the excluded person feel special in some other way ("I've been thinking you are the perfect person to shop/go to the game with").

The Waffle (or the Mysterious Maybes)

Sometimes your generous invitation is met with a hesitant, "Well, maybe I can come. I don't know yet." Or the invitee says yes, then later that week he e-mails you and tells you he actually can't come after all. Sometimes a guest will change his mind a third time, and finally, the day before your party, he will deign to accept. These folks are, for the most part, poor bet-hedgers (see page 73). What's a host to do?

If it's a dinner party, you really need to be firm with these wafflers who are waiting to see if they get a better offer, waiting to see who else is invited before they commit, or conflicted in some other way about coming. However politely you do it, you must insist they give you a definite yes or no—unless they can supply you with a darn good reason for their delay in confirming (e.g., "My dog is having an operation two days before and I have to see how he's doing. Could I possibly let you know at the last minute?"). Even if they have a valid reason, you are well within your rights to respond, "I'm so sorry! We'd better make it another time. Don't worry, I'll have another party soon." Unfortunately, with a large party you have to accept this type of tentative behavior from people you invite—and hope they show up. If they do, you must be gracious and happy to see them. But as far as I'm concerned, too much fence-sitting will eventually find you slipping off my guest list.

Note: It's hard to be too strict with people who tell you they don't know whether or not they can get a babysitter. This can be a truly difficult issue for many parents who want to socialize. However, be aware that this excuse is sometimes used as a dodge.

What to Do When People Have the Gall to Say No

There is, I'm afraid, a downside to all this politeness: It's some-times tricky to know how people really feel about seeing you. If you invite Arthur and Max to a party and they graciously turn you down (they are "busy," they are "sick," or they are "going to be out of town"), might it mean something more? How many times should you ask them over before you accept the fact that they are "just not that into you"? Again, three is the magic number.

There is a wonderful old song by Sammy Cahn from 1945 whose first line is "Kiss me once, and kiss me twice, and kiss me once again." This is what I keep in my mind for these rejections. I just think to myself, *Ask them once, and ask them twice, and ask them once again.* If after three invitations to your home they have not managed to accept one of them, it still may not mean they 1) hate you, 2) never want to come to your home, or 3) have some kind of social phobia. What it does mean is that the ball is in their court. You must cease all invites until you get one from them.

Playing Russian Roulette

Conversely, there might be someone who you don't want to invite to your party but who you feel you absolutely cannot get out of inviting. Perhaps it's a person who already knows you are planning a social event and you can't omit him from your guest list because you work together and it would be bad for your business relationship. Per-haps it's your next-door neighbor and you are hosting a barbecue to which you are inviting other neighbors. Whatever the reason, there are some cases when you may just have to steel yourself for a little Russian Roulette.

It may sound sneaky, but many of us are secretly guilty of (at least once) purposely scheduling a party for a time we are fairly sure a particular person can't make it. And yes, there is always a chance that the trick will backfire and you will end up with the unwanted guest. But remember that the very believability of this technique lies in there being some amount of risk involved. You can't hurt someone's feelings by not inviting him to the party if you did invite him—it's not your fault if he can't come, is it?

The Language of Hosting: Setting Boundaries Before the Guests Arrive

Communication is the key to almost every kind of interpersonal experience. The host/guest relationship is no different. It may seem like excessive worrying to "prep" your guests, but it is generally better to tell everyone—before they arrive—as much as possible about what is in store for them.

This tenet is for your own protection as well as for the guests. For example, if the guest has kids or pets, do not assume they will not bring them along to the dinner party just because you can't imagine doing that yourself. Tell the guest, "I hope you know you won't be able to bring your darling Snuffy along. Two of the other guests are allergic." Or include in your written invitation: "Sorry to be so 1950s, but this is an adult-only cocktail party!" Warning people about a guest who is sensitive in some area can stave off potentially awkward moments. ("Don't ask Sally about the scar on her cheek; she doesn't like talking about it.") If you are expecting a guest who just loves to play cards and always asks for a game after dinner, and you are also pretty sure the other guests (or you!) won't want to play, tell the card-player in advance: "Let's not play cards that night . . . I'd rather hear all about your recent trip. Besides, Millie and Bruce are not all that fond of cards, as I recall."

Likewise, your guests should know that you are (or are not) serving vegan fare, or that you do (or do not) have a pet or kids. When people ask if they can bring wine (and if you would like them to), tell them whether you prefer white or red. If your apartment or house is excessively cold or warm, warn them so they can be dressed comfortably. Guests should always have a general idea about who else is going to be coming to the party. Surprises might sound wonderful in theory, but most people like to be prepared. If there are time limits to the affair, naturally it is a good idea to be sure everyone knows about them. It may seem rude to tell the guests up front that they should leave by 11:00, but in the long run it is better for your relationship.

The Director: Setting the Scene, Steering the Conversation, and Making the Event a Hit

Lights, Music, Aperitifs!

The duty of a host is to put his guests completely at ease. From the moment they arrive, they should feel delighted to be in his house. While I am going to leave the food advice to the chefs of the world, here are what I see as the basic props for success.

· Give guests something to drink and/or eat as soon as possible.

· The lighting should be what I like to call Blanche Dubois lighting: soft, indirect light that makes everyone look enchanting. Otherwise well-appointed homes—with the most expensive and tasteful furnishings—can be all but ruined by a garish overhead light. If your guests look good, they will feel good.

- It's always a nice idea to have some *soft* background music—which is a great way to relax people, whether it be classical, jazz, rock, or pop. Note the emphasis on soft, as in *low volume*. When it comes to a party, being able to hear each other is as important as being able to breathe.

- If you are having a large party where people are going to be mingling, set up the bar area and the food area at opposite ends of a room (assuming you are not having servers) or, if logistically possible, in different rooms. This promotes people flow. You want to keep people moving.

Icebreaking: How to Un-Silence People

The first few minutes of any social affair can be awkward if guests are not already acquainted. No one knows quite where to begin. This is where you must take charge, grab hold of your conversational "pick," and break the ice. It is expected and required of every host to do so. Here are some sample icebreakers:

- "Helen and Gene just got back from a trip to Mexico."
- "Aaron is the friend I was talking about who plays the cello."
- "Mandy, did you know that Suzanne here makes incredible handbags? They are totally your style."

It won't always work the first time; sometimes you will have to keep chipping (or hammering) away until the conversation starts flowing freely.

Warning: Try not to use volatile topics for icebreakers. Subjects like politics (unless you are positive everyone in the room is on the same side) are obvious no-nos, but even a comment like "How about those Mets" could be a mistake, depending on the crowd. Get two sports fans talking about their favorite teams and the rest of your guests could be sitting there twiddling their thumbs for a long time.

Knitting of the Guests

Even after the ice is broken, it's up to you to continue to promote the conversational flow. You may be the best raconteur in the county, but you must be willing to take a backseat to your guests. If the perfect moment arises during your dinner party to insert one of your favorite stories, go for it; but remember your job is to make sure that your guests talk to *one another*. Many gregarious guests will be chatting away to each other like magpies the minute they are in the door, but often there is at least one inhibited guest who needs you to pull him into the fray. You must find commonalities and, putting aside your own desire to talk, point them out. A good host always sacrifices his ego for the good of the party. The party-giver's real enjoyment should come from watching his own hostly handiwork: the knitting together of his friends.

At a large party, a host should make sure that his guests are mingling. The host is, in effect, the director for the evening. After chatting with someone for a few minutes, he should lead that person over to someone else. The host doesn't merely introduce the two people, he provides them with their first bit of subject matter, in order to get things moving. Then he's off to do the same thing again for two or three other people he's spotted who aren't talking to anyone. Any conversational "singles" must be "married" by the conscientious host. A clever host will offer a shy person a job to do; he will get her to pass food or pour drinks and keep her busy with tasks that necessitate her interacting with people.

The host must make sure he spends a few moments—no matter how brief—with every single person who sets foot in his home, even if it's somebody's cousin who wasn't even invited. It helps, of course, that a host has no need of exit lines; the mere fact of his being host will allow him to say, "Excuse me," and leave in the middle of any conversation.

Hostess Interruptus

Always remember that you, the hostess, are driving this party. (If you are cohosting with your partner or roommate, you are sharing the driver's seat.) What this means is that when the party starts to veer off in any unwanted, unpleasant, or unhealthy direction, it is you who must grab the wheel and get it back on track. This usually happens when one of the guests starts monopolizing the conversation, whether because he is drunk, is an egotist, or just talks a lot when he is nervous. Usually the talker is a strong personality and may be hard to interrupt, but interrupt him you must.

The best way to use this conversational rescue technique is to imagine the talkative guest as a runaway horse. He's galloping away, taking you and all of your guests with him against your will. First you have to *stop* the runaway horse, then you have to *hand off* the reins to someone else.

" ... So the thing about my field is that it's always changing, and I've had to really scramble to keep up, but I have done pretty well, I think ... " the talker might be saying.

Now you, the hostess, need to cut him off at the pass. Don't worry about interrupting him; in this case it's your job. Interject with: "I think we all find it's hard to keep up, with so many things changing so fast." (This is the *stop*.) Then turn to another guest: "Sandy, didn't you tell me that your gallery was dumping all its artists and going for a whole new trend?" (This is the *hand off*.). With a bit of gumption on the part of Sandy, you should have someone else leading the conversation for the moment. Of course, if you have a real talker on your hands, you must be prepared to execute the Hostess Interruptus technique more than once.

Conversational Resuscitation

There may be other times when, even though the conversation has been moving along briskly for a while, it suddenly dies an unexpected death. At a dinner party, fifteen seconds of silence can seem like an eternity. Now, it's true that silence is often an unappreciated thing in our modern world, but at a dinner party silence is not golden, it's wooden. As host, you are the one who must bring the party back to life. Quick, before it's too late! You can:

- Make a toast—about anything: the season, the weather, the party, a recent triumph of one of the guests. Toasts are great little jump-starters.
- Ask your guests if they need anything. This is a good ploy because somebody is bound to want *something*, even if it's just more water, and then you can move about getting it for them. Usually movement of some kind shakes people out of their stupor.
- Make a joke about the silence, such as "I guess this silence means everyone likes the food!" People will laugh, and compliments about the food will ensue.

Playing with Guests

One way to make people relax and stop feeling self-conscious is to encourage everyone to reach down into their inner children—and play. You will probably do this without even thinking, but here are various conversational "games" you can play with your guests:

Poll Taking

You have to have willing participants, but the best way to start this fun pastime is to present a little irrelevant question, such as:

- "What color are these dishes anyway? My grandmother always called them 'the pink dishes.' Do you even see any pink?"
- "If you could eat only one thing for the rest of your life, and no matter what it was, it wouldn't make you any more or less healthy, what would it be?"
- "A friend asked me today how I would characterize his laugh. It was actually hard to do. How would you describe yours?"

Show-and-Tell

This is usually applicable only if someone at the table brings up the subject of gifts. Then you jump up from the table with a, "Wait until you see this!" and bring back to the table the funniest, tackiest, or weirdest gift you ever received (which you have kept handy for purposes of show-and-tell).

The Repeated Joke/Gag

This is the kind of play that has to happen naturally, but as host you can help it along. When something—a joke or witticism, a spoonerism, a faux pas—strikes a chord with everyone, it can become a chorus for the members of the party to keep coming back to, as if it were a reliable button to push, sure to get a laugh from the group. Often the repeated joke requires a spirit of silliness. We let our defenses down when we are silly.

When this kind of verbal play occurs, something special happens. Your dinner party becomes a playgroup. You provide the spark, but you hope that your guests will be ignited until your table is spending a lot of the evening laughing. And I believe laughter is ultimately the goal of any gathering.

Grace Under Fire

Hosting is more like being in a baseball game than being in a play. There is no script to follow. You have to hope that you're in good enough shape (the more practice you get, the better) so that when someone throws something at you, you can react appropriately and not have it negatively affect the guests or the success of the party. The test of true hosting genius is how well the host responds to events when they don't go quite as planned.

Guess Who's Coming to Breakfast, Lunch, or Dinner?

It is 11:00 A.M. on a Saturday, and Harry is getting ready to host a dinner party. There are seven guests coming, and the menu is set; in fact, two of the dishes are already prepared and cooling in the fridge. Harry is straightening up the living room when one of the guests, Gabrielle, calls.

"Harry, darling, I'm terribly sorry to impose but I've just had an unexpected houseguest land on my doorstep," she says. "May I bring him to dinner?"

What should Harry do?

a) Tell Gabrielle that he cannot *believe* she is calling him on the very day of the party to ask him a question like that, and maybe they should no longer be friends.

b) Tell Gabrielle that everything is already planned—from the pâté to the peach tarts—and unfortunately he simply won't have enough food if an extra guests comes, but that he sincerely hopes Gabrielle will be able to make it next time.

c) Tell Gabrielle that of course her friend can come—the more the merrier—but would she mind picking up a pound of smoked salmon and an extra bottle of wine before she comes?

The answer, of course, is c. One extra guest is not a terrible imposition, and it could add a new and exciting element to the party. So what if you are a little more crowded at the table? What if you do have to figure out how to split eight tarts into nine? The success of the dinner party depends not on the flawlessness and presentation of the meal, but on your guests having fun. (Of course, you do have to hope that Gabrielle's drop-in guest is as delightful as she is.)

Dealing with the Drop-In

A drop-in is different from the unexpected guest described above, because the drop-in shows up at your home without any warning at all. A very good friend of mine told me of an extreme drop-in case at her house in the Hamptons. She was having a weekend party that included a well-known author, a literary agent, and their spouses. An unpublished and somewhat desperate writer who lived nearby heard about the literary guests. He arrived in the backyard during Friday evening's cookout and never left. Every time the weekend group left the house to go somewhere, he was sitting on the back patio, reading a book. The interloper was not a total stranger, so the hosts did not feel they could flat out tell him to go home. Short of calling the police, there was nothing to be done but talk to him. All hints dropped by the host fell on deaf ears. Oddly enough, it actually enhanced the weekend because it became a joke among the guests. "I wonder if Charley will worry about us being late," one would quip. "Do you think Charley will have the sports page out there?" another would say.

Drop-ins can be an inconvenient problem; on the other hand, some spontaneous socializing can be wonderful—a surprise gift in the middle of a dreary day. Recently, as I was sitting down to some soul-killing task like paying bills, I got a phone call from a friend I had not seen in a while. She was "in my neighborhood." I invited her up for coffee and leftover cake, and it was lovely.

However, when someone shows up at your house unannounced and you are not in the mood to drop everything for the drop-in, here is a good gambit:

If there is no way to pretend you are not home, let the interloper in briefly, telling her you only have ten minutes because you: a) are just about to leave the house to go somewhere, b) are just about to have to take an important private call, or c) are not feeling well. Give her a glass of water, and tell her you will call soon to make a date.

On the other hand, according to the inimitable Miss Manners, "Under no circumstances should one let an untimely visitor cross one's threshold." So maybe you should throw your bathrobe on over your clothes and answer the door with, "Sorry, I'd ask you in but I am getting dressed. Can I call you later?"

Smoothing Over Snafus

Since it is the duty of the host to ensure the happiness of all guests, at least while they are under the host's roof, the host should step in upon the commission of an embarrassing gaffe by one of the guests. For instance, if one of your male guests should happen to turn to the woman next to him to congratulate her on her pregnancy (when she is not, in fact, pregnant), you must leap in and try to smooth things over as best you can. Here are some basic smoothing over techniques:

THE EXCUSE: Rationalize the faux pas. ("You mustn't mind Scott; he's a new parent—he's had about five seconds sleep today.") Then change the subject and get the focus off the unfortunate remark as quickly as possible.

THE ANECDOTAL ANTIDOTE: What you need for this technique is a really good faux pas story—something *you* did at another time that was *more* embarrassing than whatever it is the guest has just done. If it is entertaining, the recounting of this story will do much to dispel the embarrassment of your guest. You take the heat off the guest and put it on yourself.

THE INVISIBLE FAUX PAS: This technique is favored by most hosts for smoothing over minor mishaps. What you do is to totally and utterly ignore the faux pas. Don't flinch, don't look, don't cough. It never happened. Ignorance is bliss—at least for the guest who erred.

THE MIRROR: A true mark of courtesy, as well as courage, is for the host to casually commit the same mistake as the guest. This won't work for the pregnancy gaffe, of course, but should a guest spill a glass of wine on the table—oops—there goes your own glass! Did someone laugh when there was no joke? You merely giggle along with her.

You're Not the Nanny: Strategies for Getting Guests to Watch Their Own

I adore children. I am "Auntie Jeanne" to many a small person. However, when parents bring their kids to my house I expect them to be in charge of them, auntie or no. Sometimes parents forget that they are not in their own home, where little Johnny can run around all he wants. One man I interviewed, whose six-year-old son lives with him, told me about a dinner guest's daughter using his collection of LP records as Frisbees, while he, the host, was busy serving the dessert. Whether or not you have kids of your own, you should not be expected to be in charge of other people's children just because they are all under your roof.

A parent might say to her hostess, "Feel free to tell Tina not to throw the pillow at the cat if you don't want her to do that," as if it will be a great learning experience for both people; little Tina will learn to negotiate boundaries with an adult other than a parent, and the hostess will learn to negotiate with little Tina. (To be fair, often the parents feel Tina is more likely to listen to the hostess than to them). The problem is that a) the hostess has got her hands full—in bread dough or martini olives, and b) it is not the hostess's job to set boundaries for Tina. It should be obvious she should not be throwing pillows at the cat. It is neither appropriate nor reasonable to expect the hostess to discipline a guest's children.

Most parents are well-meaning, but some have blinders about their own children. There is no reason to assume that the visiting parents will have the same sense of boundaries or standards of behavior that you have. Parenting styles are as different as hairstyles these days. But the following techniques may help your guests to keep their kids under control:

APPEAL TO THEM/MAKE THEM AWARE: "Would you mind watching little Johnny around that glass table? I won't be able to keep an eye on him while I am making the drinks/cooking/serving" or "You'd better watch Johnny. This house is not childproofed *at all*. He could really hurt himself."

SUPPLY A PARENT/CHILD PROJECT: Give the child and parent a project to do together. For example, have your own child and the guest's child play a game (yes, the computer and television are both handy for this purpose). But make it clear that you and the other parents are in charge together.

HAVE A KID-ONLY DIVERSION READY: Have some coloring books or a puzzle on a small table in the corner of the room, someplace still within eyesight. If you put Johnny in another room, ask the parents to check on him periodically, if they are not already doing so.

Tricks to Get People to Go Home (or Stay Longer)

No matter how much you communicate beforehand, you can't always control how long the guests decide to stay. Some guests will be very sensitive to the host's need to end the party or his desire to keep it going, and others will be completely obtuse. Here are some handy strategies for extending the party or shooing the guests away.

Clean-Up

If you want the last guest(s) to leave, get up and start clearing away dirty dishes, glasses, and so on. Keep talking to the guest(s) while you are doing this (you never want to be rude) and accept his offer to help you carry things to the kitchen. Do not accept his offer to wash dishes or load the dishwasher. I never allow my guests to wash dishes as a rule, but also—and more important in this case—it can extend a guest's stay. If you are hosting as a couple, both of you must clean up to get the point across to a stubborn hanger-on. The guest will be forced to follow you around the house as you work, and this should get his blood moving enough for him to realize he overstayed his welcome. The minute he says anything like "I guess I probably should get going soon," quickly respond with, "Well, ordinarily we'd love to have you stay longer, but I have an early meeting tomorrow. Do you need a cab?"

Good Cop/Bad Cop

A great ruse for spouses, but also quite doable with roommates or siblings, this is a very common maneuver for encouraging the departure of guests. One of you plays the "good cop" while the other person is the "bad cop."

Dinner and coffee are long over. When you are beginning

to fear these people will never leave your house, the person cast as the bad cop yawns, stands up, and excuses himself with, "I'm afraid I've got to hit the hay. I'm dead on my feet. Good night, Mr. and Ms. Guest. Don't forget to let in the cat, sweetheart." After the bad cop has disappeared, the good cop then apologizes for the rudeness of her partner, while remarking how much it really *is* past his bedtime. Even a total nincompoop of a guest should get the message at this point and pack it in.

Note: A more extreme version of this strategy is Bad Cop/ Bad Cop: Both of you stand up, yawn, and say, "Sorry, we've just got to hit the sack!"

Surprise Ending

Wanting people to go home has never been my predicament; maybe this is where I got the name Miss Mingle. My problem is that I never want my guests to leave. If you are having a wonderful time and you want your guests to stay a little longer, the best trick I know of is to have something very special held back for this purpose: a delicious port or an incredibly tempting flavor of home-made ice cream. Then, when you feel the natives getting restless and you can sense they are thinking about departing, you get up quickly and say, "Oh! I almost forgot! I have this wonderful imported cheese/seventy-five-year-old Scotch/blueberry tart/ selection of chocolate truffles!" This only works if you have the special treat ready and waiting on a tray.

Note: Do not, however, try to make people stay against their will. I am embarrassed to say that when I was in my early twenties and I was an inexperienced and overzealous hostess, I would occasionally hang on to my guests at the door and wail, "Oh no, you're leaving already? Ohhh!" (thereby committing one of the Five Fatal Hosting Sins, see below). The surprise ending trick is really to get people to stay who are already conflicted about it; half of their brain thinks they should be off to bed but the other half is having a super-swell time and would love to stay longer. You're just helping the partying half win out.

The Five Fatal Hosting Sins

You are bound to occasionally host parties that aren't quite as successful as you'd like. Maybe every guest won't leave your house with the feeling that he has never been to such a lovely affair. Don't worry about it. Few people are perfect hosts every time. We learn from our mistakes. Just try not to commit one of the following serious hosting sins and you will be fine:

Sin 1: *Failing to offer the guest something to drink immediately upon his entering your abode.*
This is part of putting the guest at ease. The first few minutes are psychologically very important. It doesn't have to be fine wine or ancient Scotch—it can be ice water—but offer something right away. (You can let him sit down first, of course, though I have been know to hand my guest a gin and tonic on the doorstep.)

Sin 2: *Complaining about hosting.*
This is very bad form indeed. Many hosts do this as a result of their own nervousness. ("I'm really too tired to be doing this tonight," or "It's so hot in this kitchen; I never should have said I'd roast anything in August!") This kind of comment, even if it's how you feel, is a definite no-no. No one wants to know that you are not having a good time. (If you are not having a good time, the guests will not have a good time.)

SIN 3: *Talking about upcoming parties or events to which anyone present is not invited.*
This is rude and can be hurtful to the left-out person. If you are sitting at a café with David and George, you should not turn to David and say, "When you come to my house for dinner on Saturday, you will meet a wonderful musician I know. You'll love him!" George may be a brand-new friend, but it is still off-putting for George to have to hear about future fun events he will not be attending. This is what e-mail is for; communicate to David about your party later.

SIN 4: *Not having enough on hand to eat or drink.*
You may run out of red wine, you may not have enough cake to go around; however, you must have some kind of backup fare. Whether it's cheese and crackers, or fruit and cookies, your guests must never leave your house hungry (if they have come for a meal).

SIN 5: *Making your guests feel guilty about anything.*
This includes making them feel bad about being late, leaving early, not bringing the right thing, drinking or eating too much while they are there, making a verbal faux pas, spilling something, or even breaking something. If a guest comes an hour late, drunk, insults your other guests, spills red wine on your white sofa, breaks a vase, and leaves before dessert, you still must be as polite as possible. You can take him to task later (when he's sober). Or better yet, never see him again.

What do you get for all your hosting trouble—a medal? Better than that: It is to be hoped that if you give your friends a good time in your home, they will invite you to theirs, and in this way your friendships will deepen and your fun quotient will increase.

CHAPTER 5

Overnight Guests

THE HOUSEHOST'S HANDBOOK

W e have been going on "sleepovers" since we were little, when asking a friend to spend the night was the standard gesture of camaraderie and we never wanted our playdates to end. As adults, our "overnighters" are mostly either friends who used to live in the same city as us but have moved away, out-of-town relatives, or local friends we have invited to join us on vacation. But there are many other occasions for having (platonic) houseguests. Perhaps it's a friend whose house is being painted or whose spouse is out of town and she's lonely (or she's on the outs with her spouse). Sometimes it's an out-of-town acquaintance who needs a place to stay overnight for business—it might even be someone you've never met, a friend of a friend. Depending on where you live, you may get frequent houseguest requests from people you don't know well (but would like to know better) who are headed to your city for reunions, weddings, or other large events and looking for a place to stay. And sometimes (though mostly with girlfriends) friends decide to spend the night together even though they live across the street from each other because they simply want to stay up all night talking. (I confess I have been shushed by many a sleepy husband.)

Whatever the reason for them, sleepovers tend to foster closeness. If the act of eating together under one roof is the beginning of real friendship, sleeping under one roof often cements it. There are few better ways to really get to know someone than to spend a whole day or more of uninterrupted time together. There is shared intimacy in waking up in the morning in the same house, in experiencing each other's way of being "at home." Househosting and houseguesting are good tests of how compatible you really are. It's not always a test you both pass; sometimes you learn more than you wanted to.

One of the often-overlooked bonuses of a having a guest stay with you is that you see your life through his (rose-colored) eyes. He reminds you of all the positive aspects of your home, your lifestyle, and the area in which you live—in case you have forgotten the good points, which most of us often do. When I visit my friend in Virginia who has a pool, I help her appreciate just how very nice it is to spend time relaxing there. When she comes to visit me in New York, we go to all the museums and restaurants I take for granted (or don't take the time to enjoy). Houseguests, if they are vacationing, might also coax the host into leisure mode, inducing him into a usually much-appreciated break from his routine.

You definitely give up privacy and space for a short while when you have houseguests—it's an interruption in your life. But most of the time it is entirely worth it.

Guest Control: How to Repel Freeloaders and Get the Guests You Want

There is nothing so wonderful as a weekend visit from an old friend whom you love and miss, where you get to spend the whole wonderful two days catching up, laughing, and remembering your lives. It can be sweet, fun, poignant, and grounding. These are people who come specifically to see you. However, not all houseguests fit this description.

Should you happen to reside in a popular location, people will want to come to stay with you because they want to visit your city or area and they don't want to stay in a hotel. These can be friends, relatives, or friends of friends (or friends of friends of friends). A woman I interviewed from Washington, D.C., told me about a visit from a young man who was a friend of her cousin's, who, she was told, was coming to the city for a "very important interview." The woman put him up, as a favor to her cousin. When he arrived, it became all too obvious he just wanted a free place to stay during his spring break from college. He went out drinking with buddies all three nights he was there—with no interviews in sight.

Most houseguests, however, fall somewhere in between the categories of best friend and freeloader. One woman I know who lives in a house on the beach always has drop-in houseguests. Most of the time she welcomes them with open arms; she has a big house with many guest rooms. Her friends know to bring plenty of supplies and are prepared to fend for themselves, though this host also loves cooking big meals for everyone. Once in a while, it gets to be too much, and she decides she needs privacy and calls a moratorium on houseguests for a month or two.

Then there are those plain old-fashioned crashers—friends or acquaintances who arrive in your city (or at your door) without prior warning, hoping to stay with you. Some summers ago, an artist friend of mine in Aspen received a call out of the blue from someone who had bought several of his paintings in the past. "I'm at the airport, can you pick me up?" My friend just stared at the phone for a minute, wondering if he was having a senior moment. "What?" he said. But he is so polite—and was so bewildered—he did as he was asked and went to the airport. The crasher came back to the artist's house, unpacked his suitcase, and stayed for a week.

Sometimes crashers can end up being a great experience: It can make you feel good to help someone out, to offer a port in the storm. Once I ended up with six or seven Kazakhs (visiting colleagues of a good friend) on my living room floor for the night. Not one of them spoke English, and I speak neither Russian nor Kazakh. We all had a good time anyway. (You should have seen us trying to have a discussion in the morning, over our lemon poppy seed muffins and coffee. It was likeplaying charades!)

Usually, the younger you are, the less you mind crashers and freeloaders. It can be exciting to have a myriad of interesting visitors, each one expanding your knowledge of people and the world. Whenever you have a houseguest, it's like getting a little piece of someone else's life experience. I know someone who lived in Vienna in his twenties; he had a steady stream of Americans visiting while he was there. He didn't mind at all. He said it was fun. Would he mind now, now that he is fifty and married and managing a high-profile career? Absolutely.

The main thing is that *you* (and anyone who lives with you) should decide what level of hosting suits you. You must decide if you are host or hotel, and then be happy with your decision. Remember that there is no law that says you have to let everyone come to stay who wants to. If you are not completely into having the guest in your house, you could end up being a resentful host, which is not good for your friendship. At the same time there is also nothing to keep you from having a completely open-door policy, if that is who you are. Your lifestyle, financial situation, home space, and work life all will dictate how much you want to entertain in this way. You control who sleeps in your house. And the people in your life should respect those boundaries.

One person I talked to who lives in California told me about an old friend of his—someone he hadn't spoken to or heard from in ten years—who suddenly called him up and asked if he and his two kids could come and stay for a week so he could take his kids to Disneyland. When the host said no, that it was an inconvenient time, the friend was confused and hurt—as well as completely without another plan.

There is a big difference between Welcome Mat and Door Mat. Your friends and relatives must show respect for your boundaries. But you have to show them where the boundaries are. There are several ways to maintain guest control.

No Vacancy

Throughout the summer, a writer who lives on Shelter Island gets versions of this call: "We're going to be on the North Fork next weekend. Can we come over and stay with you for a night?" or "We're on our bikes and we're in your neighborhood. Can we come by?" He told me that after several years of playing host to more people than the Plaza Hotel, he had had enough. He felt he was working the whole time he wanted to be relaxing. Last spring he phoned everyone he knew.

"Don't think I'm being rude, but I'm no longer accepting drop-ins on the island. I am currently taking 'invitation requests' for a few weekends, but my calendar will be closed by the first of May."

If this houseguest defense seems too offensive, use one of the standard excuses: Your house is being renovated, you have a leak in the guest room, or you are going to be traveling for work. Or when potential houseguests call, you can simply say, "Life is insane right now. It's a terrible time in my life for having houseguests. I can't get into details, it's just not a good time right now."

Postponing

This is an excellent way to have the houseguest on your terms (and is also a test of how much the visit is about you!). You tell the requesting guest you would "love to see him" but that particular weekend is not good for you (which presumably it isn't). Then you invite them for a time that is convenient for you. Offer the alternative date with all the graciousness and love you can.

Don't Blow Your Nos

Let's say you have a fabulous house in Albuquerque. It has a hot tub and spectacular view of the mountains. Everyone is always vying for an invite. You have a close circle of friends who know each other. How do you say yes to one and no to another? What happens when you say, "We are redoing the kitchen and can't have houseguests," and then a mutual friend lets it slip she was there last weekend and had a marvelous time? What if you blow your nos?

This is a bit of an indiscretion on the part of the mutual friend, who should be sensitive to the fact that not everyone may be invited. However, if the uninvited guest confronts you about it, all you can do is to apologize for fibbing, assure her you really do want to have her another time, and put her on the roster for the next available weekend.

As much as I believe in white lying, it is imperative that you be careful when making up excuses—especially when your friends know each other. It's best to be as honest—and as vague—as possible.

Soliciting Houseguests

The majority of the time you will be pleased and excited about a houseguest's visit. For you and your husband to invite another couple to your house at the lake, it's a big step in a friendship; in fact, it is kind of the platonic version of sleeping together.

You will probably have to ask the couple more than once. First you might say, "Why don't you guys consider coming out to the house sometime?" See if they are into it, how they react. If they are enthusiastic, the next time the conversation comes up, start talking dates. But you will need to have a little confab about the details before they come.

Houseguest Foreplay:
Pre-Visit Information Exchange

Just as an ambassador must negotiate in advance the terms of the visit when preparing to host a foreign dignitary, it's essential that you communicate with your houseguests before they arrive. It's not only a courtesy but also an act of self-preservation to give your guests as much information as possible about their upcoming stay. You can circumvent an enormous amount of potential awkwardness and conflict, and it will be more fun for everyone.

The Guest-ation Period: How Long Should They Stay?

We've all heard the saying (generally attributed to Benjamin Franklin) about fish and houseguests smelling after three days, but this maxim is really only half true. A really great guest who has come at the perfect time—when your work is slow, or the kids are off at camp—can stay for a week and it can be more pleasurable for you than a difficult guest who has arrived at an inopportune time and stays for only one night. A visit from a couple with several very small, very active children can make half a day seem like a month. If you live in east Texas and hardly ever have houseguests, a two-week visit from good friends can feel like heaven. Yet if you live in New York City, where most people's living space is cramped and the flow of houseguests never-ending, you may want a strict two-night-only rule.

In any case, it is wise to tell people who you have never had stay over before—no matter how much you think you like them—to come for just one or two nights. Of course, the length of the visit will also depend on how much space and free time you have; it's certainly easier to have houseguests if you have a huge home with extra bedrooms. If you have a guest house, for example, you may think nothing of asking a guest to stay indefinitely. (Note: Guest houses, as luxurious as they are, do not promote intimacy in the same way, as you are not actually living in the same house as the guest.) But the best guest is welcome even in the smallest homes and the most difficult guests can be an irritant even in a mansion with a guest house.

By far the most important thing is to hash it out before the guest(s) comes. I have heard numerous stories of people who come to stay "for a few days" and settle in for a month. This is why the "foreplay" is so important. Houseguesting is really a contract between the guest and the host. The terms must be agreed upon. But the final say on the guest-ation period is up to the host. If people want to stay longer than you feel comfortable, tell them you would be glad to host them for a few days and will help them find a hotel for the remainder.

If you are smart, like my friend Greg, you organize the guests' exit at the same time that you do their entrance. "Why don't you take the 5:15 out," he might say. "That way I can pick you up after my last meeting. And, as Anne and I have to attend this darn benefit Sunday at 6:00, we'll put you on the 4:20 back to the city." *Finito.* No questions, no gray area. It's all set. It's actually very relaxing for the guest to know the boundaries.

Lay of the Land

The more information you give houseguests in advance, the smoother the visit usually goes. Naturally this information should be disseminated with some subtlety. You don't want to say to the guest, "Come for two-point-five days. I will cook breakfast only. It's cold here in November. Don't be an idiot like you were last year. Bring a coat." Instead, say, "Why don't you plan on getting here in time for dinner on Friday? Then if you leave on Sunday night, we will have all Saturday and Sunday to play! And don't forget your winter coat; it's already gotten so cold here!"

As much as you can, provide out-of-towners with clear directions to your house—if possible e-mail them a train or bus schedule, telephone numbers, etc. Let them know whether or not you will have a meal waiting for them. You should convey whether you will be cooking for them, and if you are, inquire if there are any allergies or eating restrictions. If I am visiting a family in the country I assume most of the meals will be cooked in the home (although I will offer to help shop and cook). But if it's the big city, the guest might assume otherwise. Tell the guests about the events or activities you might have scheduled for their diversion and amusement, so that they know what clothes to bring. (No matter how many times I tell people to bring good walking shoes for New York, they tend to arrive in sweet little sandals that go perfectly with their outfit but leave them with pinched, sore feet an hour later.) Let them know if you have a dog who bites or a cat who pees on the floor. Give them the heads-up if your husband tends to scream out in his sleep, or your baby girls (or you) are going to cry all night long.

It is also important to spell out what level of togetherness you had in mind. Is your idea of a perfect weekend to spend every waking moment with your guests or just some of the time? You need to say either "I'd love to show you the city" or "I'm going to be working/busy for part of the weekend, but there are so many great things for you to see." Let them know whether or not you are going to be available to show them around.

Tour Guide or Concierge?

The guests are here. You wake up and give them coffee. You begin to plan the day. Do you get out the map and show your guests where to go, or do you take them completely in hand?

I am not the only host who is often conflicted about this. Being a single person in Manhattan with a two-bedroom apartment, I have a lot of houseguests. I always complain that these guests take up too much of my time; yet at the same time, I am compulsively compelled to take them everywhere and show them New York. Much of the time they would be perfectly happy to go off by themselves. Other big-city hosts I know simply give the guests a key and send them off with a "Have fun!" No matter how much you have communicated beforehand, sometimes it is hard to get the right balance for you and the guests about how much time to spend together. Different people have different ideas about what is normal houseguest behavior. Several people I know told me that they never stay anywhere without going off by themselves for an hour or two. They feel this is good for them and good for the hosts as well.

"Guests shouldn't monopolize your time," one man told me. "You simply bring out the map at breakfast and give them directions on where they should go. Then you meet for dinner." There are many other people who expect to spend most, if not all, of the day shepherding the guests. It is generally understood that, unless prearranged, you will have meals with your guests. But better make sure before you put the roast in.

What's Mine Is Yours (Sort Of)

You want to be friends. You want to be cool. You want to be generous. But what do you do when your houseguest asks you if he can borrow your new racket to go play tennis in the rain, or take your laptop down to Starbucks to check his e-mail? What do you say when he asks if he can drive your brand-new BMW to his job interview so he will look good to his prospective employers? Just how much hospitality do you have to show?

Please Don't Touch My Computer:
The Gentle Enforcement of House Rules

Many people I interviewed told me they are too polite or embarrassed to ever refuse any request, such as the use of a personal computer, the opening of a special bottle of wine that the guest has stumbled across, or the sharing of a $90 jar of skin cream. I think this is carrying good manners too far. You are not doing the guest any favors by letting him borrow or use something if it makes you uncomfortable or resentful; it may make you less eager to ask the guest back and he will never know why.

I have a strict rule: No one but me touches my computer. Ever. Since I work at home, it is my livelihood. I made this rule after two teenage boys surfed on my computer the night they stayed with me. Not only did my computer crash, but I got porn spam for months afterward. Happily, the increasing prevalence of BlackBerrys makes the borrowing of the house computer less of an issue.

Just say no. Say it politely, make an excuse if you like ("Oh dear, that wine actually belongs to someone else" or "My computer has been acting weird, I think my hard drive is about to crash"), and offer something else to the guest right away, to take the sting out of your refusal.

How to Lend Things and Get Them Back

Upon lending an item to your guest, if you really don't care about it, you should say so. "Don't worry about getting anything on that sweatshirt, I never wear it." You should not lend anything to a guest if it is something so important to you that it would upset you not to get it back; there is no guarantee, once something is lent. However, if you *do* hope to get it back safely, don't say, "Please don't spill anything on that!" Instead suggest, "You don't have to send that back FedEx; regular mail will be fine. No rush."

Of course, frequently you will lend things to your houseguests that you never expect to get back—or that you don't even want back. Once a friend came to stay who was in town only for the day but she missed her flight. She is a good friend, and I was more than happy to let her stay the night. The next morning, as she had not brought a change of clothes, I produced—to her utter amazement—a pair of teeny, green-and-brown tiger-striped bikini underpants, which had mysteriously appeared in my clean laundry as if by magic. This came very decidedly under the heading of things you give to your guests with the phrase, "Keep it!" It became a joke between us for years after, especially as she ended up lending this very wild underwear (freshly laundered, of course) to a houseguest of *hers*.

Many things you lend will actually be gifts; upon the guests' departure you tell them to keep whatever it is, especially if it seems as if they like or need it. If you can do this, it is a very nice send-off for the guest. *What to lend*: sunscreen, hats, jackets, cheap sunglasses. *What* not *to lend*: lovers, money, or your mother's diamond ring.

Tips on How to Please Your Guests Every Time and Have Them Begging for More

Whether you give your guests a key and linens and stay out of their way or whether you take them on a walking tour of your city, if you want to be a stellar hostess you should be focused on the guests' pleasure.

Once a dear friend came to stay for a few days. The first evening I had made plans to go to a restaurant downtown I had been wanting to try. As she was unpacking and settling in, we started talking about house fires, because she had just seen a building on fire a few blocks from me. Then she told me that her own house in Boston had burned down when she was eight years old.

"That must have been so horrible for you," I said. "Did you lose everything?"

She told me she had lost all of her clothes and toys, but that the thing she grieved for most was her collection of Barbie dolls and that she mourned them to this day.

A light went on in my hostess head. Then a light went on in my closet, where I had stashed my own (substantial) collection of Barbies, which I had never found the strength to get rid of. Dear reader, I confess it, it's true: We played Barbies that evening (and ordered in) instead of going to the trendy downtown restaurant. And how happy I was to be able to give my houseguest, my friend, this bittersweet treat! We both laughed and felt like eight-year-olds again.

A good hostess does everything in her power to make the guest feel happy that she has come. You have to find the perfect balance of pleasing them and still pleasing yourself. You don't want to make yourself crazy trying to please the guest every single second. Sometimes all you have to do is prepare for the guest's comfort.

Preparation

How much should one prepare for the houseguest's comfort? I have an acquaintance who goes to great lengths to see that her guests are comfortable; she sometimes sleeps in the guest room before the guests come to make sure it has everything they might need.

Don't kill yourself cleaning. Ask yourself: When I am a houseguest, do I care about dust or do I care about the perfect nightlight and having two pillows? An exhausted, nervous hostess is worse than a relaxed, unprepared one. Don't kill yourself preparing for your guests or you won't be able to enjoy them.

Note: Procuring 600-thread-count linens, stocking special hangers in the closet, picking out coffees and teas, etc.—these are subjects I leave to the traditional etiquette and home entertaining books. It is, however, important that the windows open or the air conditioner works in the summertime, and that there are plenty of blankets in the winter.

Red-Carpet Reception

The welcome you give to houseguests is even more important than the one you give to dinner guests. These are folks who are arriving with suitcases; they can feel even more like vagabonds or scavengers. When they arrive, you must give the guests the impression you have been counting the minutes until they arrived. Even if you are finishing up some work and must delay your real welcome until you finish, be sure to tell them, "I am so glad you are here! Can't wait to catch up! Make yourself comfortable." If they have brought gifts, do not toss them aside but open them in front of the guest and make as much of a fuss as you can muster.

Foul Weathering

If you live in the city, rain is no big deal, but if your country houseguests awake to foul weather, it can make them fussy. Why not try to pretend it is a good thing? If you are not gloomy, they may not be. Books, puzzles, and games are great in the rain. Once you get into staying in, you could have the greatest time you ever had with these guests. Have plenty of good books on hand but encourage a puzzle or game. There is nothing like a good puzzle. Several people have told me that they like puzzles for house parties because they are like gathering around the fire. People focus on the puzzle and then they end up talking. Think of the rain as a good background for a great heart-to-heart conversation. Make lots of hot coffee, hot cider, hot buttered rum. Bake cookies.

Regarding Putting Your Guests to Work

I think it's impossible to visit someone in the countryside of Great Britain and not be put to work planting tulip bulbs, carrying rocks for the garden, or putting up preserves. With all due respect to the great traditions of British houseguesting, I do not believe you should put any guest to work unless it was arranged beforehand. Tell the recently arrived guest you are going to go work in the garden, and show him the hammock. If he offers to help, then hand him the shovel.

Long-term guests, however, who are staying with you for a week or more, can be put to work without any twinge of conscience on your part. They will almost certainly offer, and should at the very least help out in the kitchen.

Slumber Party! Group Houseguest Dynamics

Sometimes several houseguests coincide—either because you have all gathered for an event, or because you thought it would be fun to have a group of people for the weekend. You have to think more carefully about who you are combining than you would if it were a dinner party. You are all going to be a little family for the weekend. Will it be a fun family or a dysfunctional one? A dinner party with two out of eight people clashing is no big deal; a weekend together is a different story.

You are the den mother (or father) to all of these houseguests. Try to make sure everyone knows in advance who is going to be there. (Although sometimes a surprise visit from your brother can blow your preplanned, well-balanced house party to smithereens.) If there are going to be so many guests at your weekend house party that some will have to share rooms, do let the potential guests know this. Houseguests have different privacy thresholds; some would rather stay home than share a room.

The Ten Types of Guests and How to Handle Them

The worst houseguests I ever had broke up (as in, decided to get a divorce) at high volume in the middle of the night. The woman I hadn't known at all; her husband was the son of a friend of a friend. This kind of loosey-goosey connection is already a dangerous basis for inviting people to stay in your home. But there they were on their way to a channeling weekend in Connecticut, and they needed a place to stay in New York for one night. (What's a channeling weekend, you may ask? It's where people gather together to talk to an entity from another universe. And believe me, these houseguests of mine could have used some advice from *someone*, no matter what universe.)

I knew I was in trouble fairly early on, when the couple could not agree about where to go to dinner. As is my wont, I offered them a choice of several places in my neighborhood: Indian, Thai, Italian, French, Japanese.

"You always want Asian food," said Larry, when his wife voted for Thai.

"That's because Asian food is healthier," replied Carrie.

"Bull. You just like it because it's trendy," said Larry gloomily. "You're such a sheep."

I didn't like the way this was going, and I could feel my inner referee kicking in. "Speaking of sheep, we could always have lamb at the Greek place," I suggested with a conciliatory smile. It was a clumsy segue and it also didn't work.

"Maybe there is a *reason* the entire rest of the *whole thinking world* is eating Asian food, Larry!" snapped Carrie.

Things continued on like that for most of the night. When I at last said good night, leaving them with towels and wishes of a good night's sleep, I wondered what I had been thinking when I invited them in the first place. I breathed a sigh of relief that the night was finally over.

But of course it wasn't. At 3:00 A.M., I could still hear them arguing, and then I heard Larry yell loudly, "Look, you are being *rude* to our *hostess*! We don't even know her and you are causing a scene!" Finally I heard what sounded alarmingly like objects being thrown around the room, and, especially as the guest room was also my office, I felt I had to intercede. I knocked on the door.

"You guys?" I said, trying to put aside my outrage at being kept up all night and dragged into their nightmare of a marriage. "Is there some way I could help?" This was my way of letting them know I could hear every word they were saying (or yelling). Also, I thought as long as I was up anyway, maybe I could do something.

"STAY OUT OF IT!!" they yelled in unison.

I was never more relieved at someone leaving my home.

Few houseguests are as disruptive as the aforementioned couple. Most of your guests will be helpful, grateful, and fun to have around. But as much as you may think you know someone as a friend, you never really can tell what kind of a houseguest they might be. What follows are some tips on handling different flavors of overnight guests, which I have divided into ten basic types.

All of us have leanings toward one type or another, or are a combination of several types. If your guest is of a particular houseguest type, there are ways to make the time together in your abode more comfortable and more satisfying for you both. Some types of guests will mesh better with some types of hosts; it's a delicate and unique equation. If you are a laid-back person, a nervous guest may drive you crazy; if you yourself are high-strung, that same type of guest may suit you well.

Now let's let our ten guests in.

1. THE APATHETIC GUEST

The Apathetic Guest (otherwise known as the Guest with No Zest) is not to be confused with a lovely low-key guest who is perfectly content to sit quietly and read a book. The Apathetic Guest has no idea what he wants to do and yet does not seem particularly happy sitting around doing nothing. When you ask him what he wants to do, he shrugs and says, "I don't care." When you ask him where he wants to eat he says, "I don't care." When you ask him what he wants for breakfast or whether he wants milk in his coffee, he says, "I don't care." The extreme version of the Apathetic Guest can wear you out, as if you are walking around carrying a dead weight. By the end of the day you may feel like hitting him on the head.

Handling Instructions

As you would a two-year-old, you will need to offer the Apathetic Guest a definitive choice between two specific things. Example: "We are going out to eat. Do you want to eat at the Chinese restaurant across the street, or do you want to go downtown to a little Italian place I know?" Another way to deal with the Apathetic Guest is simply go about your regular life and let the guest tag along. If you are lucky enough to be invited to a dinner party or out with friends that weekend, ask if you might bring the guest along; you will not have to expend as much energy if you are in a group.

2. THE OBSESSED GUEST

The Obsessed Guest is the exact opposite of the Apathetic Guest. This is the guest who absolutely *must* see the Liberty Bell or get into a particular restaurant or she is not a happy camper. Heaven forbid the exhibit is closed or the restaurant isn't taking reservations on the day she comes—you will never hear the end of it. Often inflexible by nature, the Obsessed Guest will talk nonstop about the object of her obsession, and will stop at nothing to achieve her goal.

Handling Instructions

This type of guest can be great fun if you happen to share her obsession—for example, if both of you *must* see the Biennial exhibit at the Whitney or die trying. How to handle the obsessed guest otherwise? You could try telling her beforehand that the object of her obsession will not be possible; then if you do manage it, she is pleasantly surprised. Of course the best, most obvious thing to do is to fulfill the obsession as soon as humanly possible.

3. THE GUEST WHO WON'T GET DRESSED

It's the naked truth: There are guests who come to your house and sit around in pajamas or a robe—or even their underwear—for a large part of their stay. Now this is not a bad thing if you happen to be the kind of person who simply loves finding a dozing guest in a silk muumuu on your divan at all hours of the day. However, most hosts will want the guest to get dressed and get the heck out of there so they can make something of the day. In this category of guest is the person who sleeps very late, or just lazes about as if they have come to your house merely to sit on your couch. A neighbor of mine told me, "I have an old friend I love but when he comes to my house he sleeps until noon, then he sits around reading the paper until 2:00. I feel as if I am being pulled into sloth!" The host may not feel comfortable with just leaving the guest there dawdling while he goes about his day.

Handling Instructions

Besides asking the guest if he might need some help in locating his clothes, you could try one of the following:

· Scare him: Tell him a friend is about to drop in.
· Lure him: Tell him you have a surprise to show him (outside the house and it won't last forever!).
· Give up on him: Leave the guest with snacks, the remote, and your cell phone number, should he rouse himself later.

4. THE DEPRESSED GUEST

It goes without saying that any guest who comes to avail herself of your hospitality and is horribly depressed is a downer at best and a disaster at worst—unless, of course, it's a really good friend and you are actually able to help her. A garden-variety case of depression can be okay, but the super-stressed-out guest (overworked, jet-lagged, or on the verge of a nervous breakdown) is a little harder to deal with, as are couples or families who are fighting.

Handling Instructions

Concentrate on distractions and on soothing surroundings. Don't go to loud bars or crowded venues. Take the guest on quiet walks, provide lots of fresh air and comfort foods, and lend a sympathetic ear.

5. THE GRUMPY GUEST

Unlike the Depressed Guest, who is just going through a rough time, the grumpy guest is grumpy by nature. This is someone who habitually wakes up on the wrong side of the bed (and usually doesn't make it, either), grumbles about the weather, and looks at the glass of life as half full.

Handling Instructions

Why you invited the Grumpy Guest in the first place, I don't know. But now that he is there, your best course of action is to just go ahead and be grumpy with him. Try it. See if you can out-grump him. Agree with him that life sucks. You may find him cheering up a bit, just to be contrary.

6. THE MESSY GUEST

I personally do not mind the Messy Guest at all—provided the mess is contained in the guest room. But I am a cluttered enough person on my own that if I have to continually sort out my shoes, magazines, and toothbrush from the guest's, it begins to frazzle me.

157

Also, many hosts will find it unsettling to look in the wide-open door of the guest room and see an unmade bed and clothes on the floor.

Handling Instructions

Try one of the following lines:

- "I've put these hangers here in case you need to hang anything up."
- "You might not want to leave things on the floor. It's totally up to you, but my cat will be all over them."
- "Here you go: I found your bag of souvenirs and your five magazines and your shoes in the living room. Thought you might like to keep everything together so you won't forget stuff."

7. THE FINICKY OR CRITICAL GUEST

I'll never forget the time a friend from London came to stay. He insisted on cooking me breakfast, then proceeded to criticize my pots and pans, my kitchen utensils, and my brand of butter. I have sometimes heard this referred to as the "Why-Don't-You Guest," as in, "Why don't you have a bigger vegetable steamer?" "Why don't you have a place to put the suitcase?"

In addition to this type of guest there is the flinger of passive-aggressive insults. For example, the guest will feel your upholstery and, with a piercing look, produce a fake compliment: "What a nice couch—what *is* this material, my dear? I don't think I've felt anything quite like it." Or, upon your serving him pie, he might say, "I really liked that cake you had last time." Critical guests will snoop inside your medicine cabinet and ask you why you are taking iron pills when they are bad for you. Fussy or finicky guests will ask you if you have Pellegrino water instead of tap, and is there possibly a goose down pillow in the place?

Handling Instructions
Try to ignore all the criticism. Let it fall over you like rain. You are the host. Firm statements like "This is the way I like it" or "To each his own" may be effective. Send him out for errands to get him out of your hair as much as possible. If it gets too bad, ask him if he might be more comfortable going to a hotel. Have the number handy.

8. THE NERVOUS GUEST
If I fall into any of the ten categories, I confess I may, on occasion, be this kind of guest. The Nervous Guest hovers over the host, asking way too many times, "Can I help? Can I do anything?" The nervous guest, in her heart of hearts, is not completely convinced she should really be there at all. Perhaps she is imposing. Perhaps the host would rather she hadn't come! In its extreme form, this kind of guest can be truly irritating to the host. In fact, sometimes she can be the Guest Who Is a Pest.
Handling Instructions
The best thing to do with the Nervous Guest is to a) assure her that you are glad she is there and b) go ahead and give her a small task—ideally, one that has to be done repeatedly throughout her stay—such as the dishes, setting the table, or walking the dog.

9. THE EXPENSIVE GUEST
In 1617 in England it was rumored that Sir Richard Shuttleworth set his house, Gawthorpe Hall, on fire, rather than have to suffer the expense of King James and all his entourage coming to stay.

The Expensive Guest is the guest who comes to the city and insists you all go to dinner at a trendy restaurant and the latest Broadway show, but does not pick up the tab for you. He's not used to taking a bus, so of course you chauffer him around (with your gas) or pay for taxis. The Expensive Guest usually has no idea he is costing you money you don't have. He is not a freeloader, just a well-off friend who is not sensitive to the fact that you are not willing, or not able, to spend that kind of money.

Handling Instructions

Most people work this out in advance. But if need be, try one of the following lines, when plans are in the offing:

- "That's too rich for my blood."
- "Why don't I show you my neighborhood restaurant?"
- "Oh, I'd much rather cook for you!"

10. THE TAKEOVER GUEST

Whether it's a guest who arrives with her whole electronic office, which she proceeds to set up all over your house so she can work the entire time she is there, or a guest who rearranges your furniture and invites all her friends over for dinner, the Takeover Guest is not only stressful but also vaguely insulting. Why is the guest here, you wonder, if she is only trying to re-create what she has at home? What about what you have to offer?

A few years ago, a houseguest of mine (a friend's boyfriend, whom I had never met before) decided to hold a dinner party in my house. Insisting that I needed pasta bowls, which I didn't have, he instructed me to go out and buy them. I refused, but there was a lot of tension. The bossy guest will tell you what to wear and what you are both going to do while he is there. I even heard of one man who, arriving unexpectedly and inconveniently at his host's L.A. apartment a day early, proceeded to unpack and stow several crates of exotic snakes in the guest room. He was scheduled to be on a local TV show about wildlife. Talk about your uninvited guests!

Handling Instructions
This is, for me, the toughest one. You can either a) let the Takeover Guest take over, and have fun with the reversal of roles (with you as guest) or b) tell him you are the boss and to stop pushing you around. (Either way, you might want to be busy the next time he wants to stay.)

Have no fear! For the most part, your guests will be polite, happy, gracious, appreciative, fun-loving, generous, satisfied, and in tune with you and your surroundings. Your home will feel happier from having had them. Spending time with friends or relatives in your home, sharing your life in this way, will move most relationships forward. You learn a lot about each other through houseguesting; it's one of the ways you build lifelong friendships.

CHAPTER 6

Great Guesting

Hosting and guesting are like yin and yang—two sides of the same coin. In fact, the word "hospitality" originates from the Latin *hospes*, which can mean either host or guest. Like leading and following, the terms host and guest presuppose the existence of each other. It's a symbiosis. Just as you cannot have a game of catch without one person throwing and another catching, and you cannot have a conversation without someone talking and someone listening (unless, of course, you are at my family dinner table, where everyone is talking!), there can be no host unless there is a guest.

In general, the best guests make the best hosts, and vice versa. Aren't the best restaurant customers the ones who have worked as waiters, and the best writers the ones who read a lot? All areas of relationships and communication are like this—two aspects of the same thing that are inseparable and are inversely connected. The best guests make a host happy to be a host; the best hosts make a guest happy to be a guest.

The first duty of a guest comes before he even enters the party—in dealing with the invitation.

Fielding Invites

How to Get Invited

It's obvious that the best thing to do to get invitations is to be an exceptionally interesting and nice person, and to invite people to your own home as much as possible. (Invite unto others as you would have them invite unto you.) You need to be the kind of person people want to be around and be the perfect guest at any affair. But besides attaining personality perfection, is there anything else you can do?

Hint-Dropping

Sometimes it's advantageous to let a new friend or acquaintance know that you are interested in seeing where he lives and/or meeting his mate or children. (You can even tell him you want to see his etchings.) This may make him think of putting you on his guest list for his next affair. If you have heard he is in fact having a party on an upcoming Saturday night, and you suspect your not being invited is more about being accidentally overlooked than intentionally passed over, you can try, if it's your style, a line like, "What are you guys doing on Saturday?" or "Why doesn't someone give a party? Don't you think this time of year we really need one?" Okay, it may not be the most elegant MO, but it can be worth it if the host answers, "Oh! We're actually having a thing on Saturday! I'm sorry I didn't think of inviting you before—do come."

Getting Someone Else to Invite You

This is a little more dignified; it's like having an agent. In this case your agent is a mutual friend who is already on the guest list and agrees to check with the host to see if he can bring you. However, this can put the friend in an excruciatingly awkward position. If the host says no, the friend now has to tell you the hard truth, or try to save your feelings by prevaricating.

To Go or Not to Go

When should you go to a party you are invited to? The answer is: almost always. Go even if you won't know a soul, go if you have nothing to wear, go if you are tired, go even if you are worried your ex might be there. Life won't come to your door, and you never know who you might meet unless you go. Go even if you were invited by accident.

The only exceptions are times when you get a really bad vibe about a social event, and in those cases you should listen to your instinct. For instance, if you are invited by someone other than the hostess, be wary. ("Oh, my sister-in-law won't mind at all if you come, even if it is a formal sit-down dinner that's been planned for six weeks. I want you there! Come!") I once threw caution to the wind and accepted an invitation to a party where I knew the host did not like the person I was coming with. I figured it would be a crowded party and the host wouldn't notice. But when I arrived on the arm of the aforementioned disliked guest, I got the cold shoulder.

A Word (or Two) About the R.S.V.P.

Failing to R.S.V.P. to a written invitation, when such response is requested, is nothing but pure selfishness. It is like saying, "Even though you took the trouble to mail me an invitation and you like me well enough to be at your party, you are not worth an e-mail or phone call from me." For one thing, the host needs to know how many guests to expect. He also would like to know that a) you received the invite (that it hasn't gotten lost at the post office or in your spam folder) and b) you appreciate being invited.

Forget to R.S.V.P. too often and you many find people forgetting to invite you.

Guesting as an Active Verb

Being a guest may seem like a passive role, but it really isn't. Remember the third law of hosting: It's the guest's responsibility as well as the host's to make the event a success. It's not enough to accept an invitation and then just show up and sit on someone's couch like a passenger being taken on a trip. You, as the guest, are integral to making the experience fun, positive, entertaining, and rewarding for all. It's a team effort. You have to help to manifest whatever the host has in mind. Think of it this way: In ballroom dancing, the man may lead but the woman works just as hard (or harder) in following him. If she were not doing her part they would both fall down in two seconds flat. It is your host who is leading the dance, but you must actively participate.

As important as it is for the host to welcome the guest, you as a guest must also let the host know that you are thrilled to be there and that there is nowhere else you would rather be. Upon your arrival, tell the host how wonderful it is to see him, how well he is looking, and how much you have been looking forward to coming. Exude contentment at being there, as if you have been let into a special sanctuary, where nothing but pleasure awaits you.

After you are settled in, don't just sit there, watching it all as if it were a movie. Participate! Ask questions, make observations, introduce yourself. If the hostess is trying to break the ice and she throws out a line, pick up on it. Do some icebreaking of your own. If one of the other guests makes a joke that doesn't go over, or makes an embarrassing faux pas, do your part to try to smooth things over.

You may have your own ideas about when each course should be served, or could think of a more comfortable seating arrangement. But you are the guest, so it is your job to follow the host's lead. Go with the flow. Put your own need to control aside and go in the direction the host is leading you. You may, of course, refuse to partake of the rock candy the host puts out with the coffee. But you must never say, "Rock candy? Don't you have cookies?"

One of the other responsibilities of a really good guest is to offer to help. Keep your eye on the hostess and be sure to lend a hand whenever she seems to have too many tasks at once. If the hostess refuses your help, do not insist. She might have a good reason for wanting to do it herself. Don't make a big deal about it so that it draws attention to your offer.

Loving the Host: About Praise, Gifts, and Apologies

Remember that part of your job as guest is to make the host feel wonderful about whatever is going on. When someone invites you into her home, in a certain sense she is opening herself up to you. She is giving of herself, trusting you to like who she is, sharing the things that she likes best, hoping that you will like them too. She is the one taking the risk and being generous. Much of the host's motivation is for acceptance and praise, so you have to make her feel good even if you have to—hold on to your hats, ladies and gentlemen—lie.

In many of my books I have written about lying for the common good. People always seem to take umbrage with it, as if dedication to the absolute truth could ever be more important than being loving. In any case, you will probably only be exaggerating, not lying, when you flatter the host, telling him that the house looks wonderful, he looks wonderful, the food is fabulous, and it may just be one of the best parties you've ever been to.

If the food isn't quite up to your gourmet standards, don't let on. If you didn't have such a great time meeting the host's friend from work, lie and say you did. Sometimes *not exactly* telling the truth is what friends are for.

Gift Giving 101

In spite of all the books and articles published on the topic of gift-giving, many guests are not sure about exactly the right way to give gifts. If you want to learn all there is to learn in this area, you can consult Emily Post. But here are a few quick pointers:

· If no one else has brought a gift, be sensitive to the other guests as well as the host. Don't embarrass anyone else by making a showy presentation of the gift. Give it to the host quietly in another room or stick it somewhere and tell her you've left it.

· If you think the hostess suspects a regift: Deny, deny, deny. Say, "I have one of these, too. I like it so much I bought one for you!"

· If everyone except you has brought the host a gift (this can happen with birthday parties that specify "no gift" but no one pays attention to it), do not say, "Oh, I forgot my gift!" Don't say anything. Don't draw attention to your non-gift state. Later, if you want, you can send the hostess a "thank you for the party" gift.

· Bringing wine is almost always appreciated, but remember that the host is under no obligation to serve the wine that you bring. He might have special wines he has preselected or will end up serving wine brought by other guests. This can be frustrating if you have gone to some trouble and expense in picking out the wine, but know that the host will certainly enjoy it later. Remember, it is a gift.

Apologies

While you can never thank a host too much, you can apologize too much. If you have just tipped over an entire bottle of wine, you should apologize very sincerely and offer to make it up to the host in any way you can. But the guest who won't stop apologizing compounds the original injury; soon the apology itself begins to feel like a burden, as if the host is now not only responsible for replacing the wine you just spilled but also must help you with your guilt. An overly apologetic guest grates on the nerves as much as the Nervous Guest does. If it was a fairly minor mistake, saying "I am so sorry!" once or twice is all that is necessary. If it was a big boo-boo (such as a broken antique), it is appropriate to include in your hand-written thank you note: "And again, I am so sorry to have broken the vase. Please do send me the bill." Or joke, "I'll understand if you cross me off future guest lists," and then drop it.

How to Treat Pets and
Children Belonging to the House

Children and pets, no matter what your predilection for either, should be treated as unique treasures, which they almost always are. Your behavior in this area could be the difference between getting invited back and not getting invited back. Never take it upon yourself to discipline the children or pets of your host(s), no matter how tempted you are, even if they dump grape juice in your lap or lick your face (hopefully the licking one is the dog). Do what you must do for the preservation of your self and your clothes. In other words, act in self-defense only.

Take your cue from your host. If the host wants the children to be a part of the party, engage them, talk to them as if they are adults (except without profanity). On the other hand, if the host is trying to situate the children in another room so he can focus on entertaining, don't impede the proceedings by insisting on some quality time with the kids. Don't feed the animals (or children) from the table unless expressly encouraged to do so by the hosts. It's nice to bring a gift to the kids, and parents appreciate it; however, if there is any question about the appropriate nature of the gift (a BB gun, black lingerie), check with the parent beforehand!

Naturally, if you are good enough friends with the hosts to be considered one of the family, none of the above rules apply—except for the rule about treating kids/pets as special treasures.

Note: If you are allergic to the host's pet, you should probably come prepared with an inhaler, Benadryl, or other remedy. Bear up as much as possible, and if you must, excuse yourself and say you are not feeling well. If you are really suffering and it seems as though it would not be too much trouble for the dog or cat to be put in another room, you might risk an, "I'm so sorry, I love your cat so much, but I forgot to tell you I'm allergic." Whatever you do, do not act as if it is somehow the host's fault, that he has asked you over with the express purpose of torturing you with animal dander.

Double-Booking and Other Risky Behavior

Double-Bookers Beware
Double-booking, double-dealing, double-crossing, double whammy: all are suspect in my book. None have a positive connotation.

Perhaps you have committed to going to a friend's baby shower, from 5:00 to 8:00 on Friday. The Wednesday before, an influential man you've been wanting to get to know better asks you to his cocktail party the same night. You are tantalized, and torn. You are definitely expected at the baby shower, but you'd so much rather go to the cocktail party. So you do it: You double-book, figuring you can go to the cocktail party first and still get to the baby shower in time to see most of the presents opened. So far, so good. But then you make your fatal mistake: You tell the hostess of the baby shower that you may be late because you have to "stop by" another party before you come. To make matters worse, you stay at the cocktail party longer than you intended, get stuck in traffic, and arrive at the shower at 7:15.

Hedging your bets is one thing, but double-booking is a reckless practice unless the time of the parties only overlaps slightly. It's only human to want to have your cake and your cocktails, too. But there are times in life when, as adults, we have to make a decision and stick to it. You have to keep the health of your friendships in mind (after all, that is what all this hosting and guesting is about). You don't want to hurt a good friend's feelings just so you can have a fun evening. If you must double-book, have the decency not to tell anyone you have done so. When you get to the shower, apologize profusely and make up a good excuse for your lateness. A friend will have to forgive something that was out of your control. On the other hand, a friend may not understand your showing up for dessert with, "I couldn't get away from this other party! I mean, they had belly dancers, man!"

Imposing (or How to Crash a Party Without Breaking Anything)

You have not been invited. Yet you have heard it's going to be a huge, once-in-a-lifetime party. Everyone you know will be there. Can you crash? Should you?

Don't quote me, but if you are brave enough, you can try to slip in without anyone seeing you. Or you can show up boldly at the door and act confused when the hostess wonders why you are there. ("You invited me, don't you remember?") According to a man I know, Brian, who is thirty-five years old and lives in San Francisco, crashing is *de rigueur*. He always brings a bottle of something expensive and dresses impeccably. Within five minutes, the host wonders why Brian wasn't on his guest list in the first place.

Extra, Extra! Bringing Uninvited People

Sometimes it can't be helped. You really want to go to a party and houseguests land on your door. Or you believe that the party really needs these fabulous people; that your friends will liven it up; that you are benefiting the host by bringing them. This can be okay if it is a large party and you get the host's permission. What is not acceptable, however, is to bring ten people, eat and drink a lot, and bring nothing with you—unless you really do not have any interest in pursuing a friendship with the host.

When to Sing or Otherwise Share Your Talents

Everyone knows you are the life of the party. So naturally when you are invited to the Brawleys' dinner you bring your autoharp so you can entertain everyone. The problem? Nobody asked you to play the autoharp or anything else.

You must be asked—no, begged—to perform in any way at someone else's party. Do not simply stand up and start juggling. Any request for you to share your talents must come from the hostess (or at least be seconded wholeheartedly by her).

Contrarily, if you suspect the host has invited you because you are a professional hypnotherapist and she wants you to hypnotize the guests after dinner for entertainment, you are well within your rights to decline, unless the host makes it part of the bargain and has, in effect, hired you for the evening. ("I'm having several people over for dinner, will you come and bring your Tarot cards?") You should not be required to sing for your supper.

Having an Exit Strategy

Let's say you are invited to what you think is going to be a large cocktail party. You set out, innocently expecting a pleasant, if not quite ecstasy-filled evening, and—yikes! The host ushers you into a room where there are only six or seven people, none of whom you know. Everyone is sitting stiffly in chairs, talking in great detail about leveraged buyouts. Even though this is not a subject that interests you, you make up your mind to enjoy yourself. But after about thirty minutes, you are miserable; it is apparent that there are no other people coming, and no other topics of conversation coming, either. You can't just get up and leave, lest you offend the host. You are stuck like a lobster in a trap.

Many people won't go to parties because they are afraid of getting stuck. This is a shame because the event could turn out to be a fine time, and you really never know until you get there. Having an effective exit strategy is empowering. You will have less fear about accepting invitations.

When you are invited and it is uncharted territory, the smart thing to do is to plan your escape in advance (unlike what many governments do when going into uncharted territory!). Tell the host, when you R.S.V.P., "I would love to come, but I have to warn you that I have a tango lesson" (or "I have to take a conference call from Tokyo" or "I have to pick up someone at the airport"), "so I can only stay for a little while." If the party turns out to be wonderful, you can always change your mind and pretend to cancel whatever it is ("Oh, who cares about the tango!") or that it canceled you ("My Tokyo call was rescheduled"). On the other hand, if it turns out to be a social quagmire, you have an easy escape route in place.

The Five Fatal Guesting Sins

In spite of my detailed instructions, you really should not worry too much about all the techniques for being a good guest. Just be sensitive to your surroundings and try not to commit one of the five fatal guesting sins, and you will live to see another party:

SIN 1: *Not showing up.*
That is, without calling to say what happened. Preferably you will call beforehand to say you won't be able to make it. If it is a dinner party, better have a steel-clad reason for not coming. And if you were wondering, "We were too tired" is not good enough.

SIN 2: *Leaving before the main event.*
Unless your exit strategy is already in place (see page 173), it is poor form indeed to leave a dinner party before dinner is served, a birthday party before the cake and presents, or a wedding before the toast. Obviously if something urgent comes up, you may leave. But saying "Hey, gotta go, didn't realize you were serving grilled chicken" is not okay.

SIN 3: *Ruining/breaking things without apologizing.*
Accidents happen. Accidents without apologies should not. Any-

one can knock over a lamp. Usually the perpetrator feels worse than the owner of the ruined property. Any host worth his salt and pepper will accept a sincere "I'm so sorry!" However, if you were drunk when you broke the lamp, and as a result you don't remember the crime, that's no excuse for not apologizing; in fact your apology should be double strength.

Sɪɴ 4: *Making the host feel bad about the party.*
This includes being critical or negative about any aspect of the party, insulting the host or other guests, or making jokes about how awful the party is.

Sɪɴ 5: *Failing to thank the host.*
Even if you had a terrible time, you must thank your hosts. Always call or e-mail the hosts after you have been to their house for a large party. And when you have been to someone's home for dinner, I am of the opinion that you should send them something through the regular mail (snail mail), be it a thank you note, a fun postcard, or even a small gift. Do you feel that using the post office is a lot of bother? Exactly. E-mail takes ten seconds, and therefore does not show the amount of gratitude you need to after the amount of effort the host has put out for you. Of course, the best thank you for your host is a reciprocal invitation from you.

The best thing about being a guest at someone's home is that while is deepens your relationship with the host, it also affords you a very good chance of improving your social life. Your "co-guests" represent the best potential friends you can come in contact with, besides people at work. This is just another reason why you should try to be the best guest you can. Good guesting leads to better friendships.

CHAPTER 7

Staying Over

THE HOUSEGUEST'S HANDBOOK

Congratulations! You've become good friends with Amy and Bill, and they have (oh, joy!) invited you to their beach house for the weekend. Pack your bathing suit and your toothbrush, but also pack something else: your dedication to being the perfect houseguest. Remember, each at-home entertaining experience is an equation between you and the host(s).

The perfect houseguest is flexible, complimentary, helpful, enthusiastic, appreciative, and visibly comfortable and in tune with her surroundings. The perfect houseguest is a happy houseguest. Sound daunting? It will help to know as much as you can about your temporary home before arriving.

Research and Reconnaissance: Preparing for Your Comfort

If you have never stayed with these friends before, it will help to do a little gentle digging so that you have some idea what to expect. Try to find out what, if anything, is planned for the weekend so you can bring everything you need. As "cool" as it may seem to arrive with only a wallet, expecting nothing and ready for anything, few people over the age of twenty-one can pull it off. (You may be very "cool" indeed if you didn't realize it's freezing on the host's porch at night.)

Most people bring their own laptops these days, but if using a computer is going to be crucial to you and you're not planning on bringing your own, you should ask whether or not you can use the host's. Otherwise, assume you can't. Try not to borrow things while you are there; a good host will protest that he "lives to lend things to people he loves," but it will be less work for him if you don't have to bother him with borrowing.

Tell the host before you come if you have any special food requirements—but only if you think they will be an issue. If you are going to a beach house and you are allergic to shellfish, this is something to tell the host. If you can't digest blueberries, you can keep that one to yourself, and just skip them if they are served.

Most important, ask the hosts what you can bring. If the hosts say "nothing," do not accept that at face value. Instead, make a suggestion about what you might provide. If they insist, "No, just bring yourselves," you should *still* show up with something, especially if you are going to a vacation (secondary) home, where it is unlikely the place is going to be fully stocked. At the very least, arrive with a bottle of something, or flowers.

Host/Guest Scheduling Issues

As a good guest, you should make every possible effort to arrive when you say you will. Not earlier, not later. You may be laid back as a host and not care when people show up and you may think your hostess doesn't really care either; however, for all you know she may want to have a quick fling with the doorman before you come and she needs to know whether she can fit it in. Or maybe she just wants to be able to figure out exactly how much time she has between working and your arrival, so she can clean the bathroom.

Generally, you should never stay more than three nights. But let your hosts set the dates. If you have to be in a city for a week, say you'd love to stay the weekend and then tell the hosts you are going to check into a hotel. If the hosts demur, you should say, "Thank you, but I couldn't possibly impose." If the hosts insist, you may, if you think your friendship can stand it, concede.

If you are visiting from very far away—another country or even an opposite coast, it is also more acceptable for you to stay longer than three nights. Just be careful you don't start to overstay your welcome.

Invitation Geiger Counter (How to Detect a Fake Invite)

More than we might think, people toss around vague invitations as part of their conversation. "You must come see us at our houseboat on the Seine" may be just a way for the speaker to let you know that he has a houseboat on the Seine. He may have no concrete thoughts of actually hosting you there. (In other words, it could be a glorified "Let's have lunch.") In most cases, with people you don't know intimately, you should wait until they ask you repeatedly and start talking dates.

Similarly, your host's "Sure, we'd love to have you stay for a few more days" may be mere politeness. If you are visiting someone in the South, you may have trouble discerning the host's true import. It's a cliché, but southern hospitality can be confusing as well as charming. Again, the key is to refuse at first, and see if the host insists.

Doors, Bathrobes, and Bedtime: How to Have Privacy in Someone Else's Home

There are some areas of houseguesting that walk a thin line, and this is one of them. I myself like coming down to breakfast in my nightgown or bathrobe; to me, it's part of the intimate one-of-the-family feeling that is a big part of the experience. But many others are horrified at this notion. I talked to one woman who, when she is a houseguest, not only dresses for breakfast but never leaves her room without putting on her makeup.

Some hosts will never knock on the guest's closed door. Some guests will stay up watching TV or snacking in the kitchen after the host has gone to bed.

There are no absolute rules here except one: You have to *read the household.* Is it a bathrobe kind of house? Is it a closed-door kind of house? Is it the kind of house where the guests are expected to help themselves to food in the refrigerator? Is this the kind of household where it all works better if you disappear from the house for a while and give the hosts some privacy? The only way to know is to try to pay attention, pick up on clues, and when in doubt, ask.

The Houseguest Umbilical Chord

You may not want to be underfoot. You may have other plans. But you must always keep in touch with your host and let her know your schedule. Don't disappear in the morning, leaving your host clueless about your schedule and if and when you ever plan to return. The host may need to make her own plans. Most hosts assume some responsibility for their guests. Never leave the host hanging, wondering whether or not you are going to have dinner with her, or come home at all.

Basic Houseguest Etiquette

What follows is not really etiquette in the strictest sense of the word. Etiquette instructs us about the correct way to eat an artichoke, but it is more important to make the person eating the artichoke feel good about however he is doing it. Good manners are about being loving to each other. Some of these are minor things, but if you forgo the small niceties in life, where does it end?

Here are a few basic houseguest rules to consider:

· Unless the bed is wet from a leak in the roof or is covered with tarantulas, sleep where you are told to sleep.

· If the host wants to show pictures, you must look at them.

· Be neutral in hosts' fights. Never take sides.

· Don't be nosy: Don't go into the medicine cabinet, drawers (other than those specified for your use), or closets.

· Follow the host's instructions for how to leave your room when you depart. I spoke to one man who owns a large country house and so naturally has many houseguests during the summer. "Guests should know how to leave their rooms," he admonished. "The bed should be stripped, the sheets folded roughly at the foot, with the bedcovers remade. The guests should leave as little work as possible for the host." He also suggests that guests bring their own sheets—then they just take them home, leaving the room exactly as they found it. However, other hosts I talked to disagree. Everyone has their own style. The only rule is to ask the host how he would like you to leave the room.

· No one likes to talk about this, but the rule for the toilet in the middle of the night is to flush unless instructed not to.

· Never ask for something you know the host will have to go out for, without offering to go yourself.

· Don't sleep much, much longer than the host does (as in, four hours longer).

· Always offer to do the dishes or any other simple household chore. Even better, do it without asking.

· Offer a meal. In general, you should offer to take the host out or help cook a meal.

· Always, always send a thank you—a call at the very least. A written note is better; a small gift better still.

Sex and the Houseguest

I took an unofficial poll on this ticklish subject. The majority vote is in: Couples should not have sex when they are staying overnight at someone else's house.

Wait—before you throw down this book! What I really mean by that is that you can't have loud sex or obvious sex. In general, it is disconcerting for the hosts—or other guests—to know when the houseguests are having sex. If the house is big, or the walls are thick, or you are as quiet as mice, go for it.

A good friend of mine protested when I told him this rule. "Hey, send those sexually active guests over to my house!" he said to me. "My wife and I could use the inspiration!" He felt that guests having sex in his house would put good, loving energy in it. I still say that's fine, but... *shhhhhhhh.*

The same rule applies to the hosts, as well as to a host having sex with a guest. If you are having a large house party and everyone is sneaking into everyone else's room to have sex, that's fine; but just be polite about it, which means being discreet. (Also, I'd like to be invited next time.)

How to Win the Best Guest Award

The basics are one thing, but why not shoot for perfection? The Best Guest is what I call the Bulletproof Guest. Nothing seems to negatively affect him. The subway system can break down, they can cancel all the Broadway shows, the museums may be closed, and it rains all weekend, but the Best Guest still manages to have a good time. Here are some other qualities of the Best Guest:

· The Best Guest brings his own alarm, should he need to get up for a plane or meeting. The Best Guest does not require the host to wake him up.

· The Best Guest is unobtrusive, has packed lightly, and is flexible about plans.

· The Best Guest adores your cats or kids, and often brings them presents.

· The Best Guest, when asked how she slept, always responds with "Beautifully!" Never, "It was too hot (cold/noisy/dirty)."

· The Best Guest not only brings the host a gift when he comes, he also sends a gift afterward—something the guest realized was missing from the house, or something the guest and host discussed or laughed about during the visit.

· The Best Guest never uses the host's phone or computer, unless it is an emergency. He doesn't borrow your phone charger or your electric razor.

· The Best Guest offers to wait on the host, rather than asking him for a drink. (The Best Host won't let you, but the Best Guest offers anyway.)

The Ten Types of Hosts and How to Handle Them

When you are in someone else's home, the dynamic can be tricky; no matter how subtle, the host has a certain amount of power over the guest. You are, after all, on foreign soil, hoping for good treatment. Most of your househosts are going to make you feel well taken care of. Many of your hosts are people that you already know well; you are likely to know what to expect. But for those times when you are up against a househost quality that is a little challenging, here is a guide (many of your hosts will have a little bit of several of these types):

1. THE LAID-BACK HOST (OR THE MILQUETOAST HOST)
Your hosts seem glad to see you, but they do not change their rhythm, their routine at all. They have planned nothing in particular. They say hello and go about their business.
Handling Instructions
You are either on your own or you can ride along while they pick up the kids, go to soccer practice, or do the laundry. I actually love going to visit someone in the suburbs for this kind of visit; it is such a novelty for a city chick like me. I love being driven around in a vehicle that's not a taxi—and not having to make too many decisions. I eat what is put in front of me, and help tuck the kids into bed. But it's not everyone's kind of visit.

Should you want a little more excitement, you should make suggestions for things to do or, better yet, have made some plans in advance. These types of hosts are usually extremely nice, so feel free to ask them for directions to the nearest museum.

2. THE "LET'S GO!" HOST
The Let's Go Host may remind you of the camp counselor you

had when you were ten. The Let's Go Host wants to pack as much as possible into every hour. He is probably exceedingly proud of his town and wants to show you everything. He does everything Host Haste.

Handling Instructions

This kind of host is fun but can get exhausting. Be sure to ask the host for a time-out. ("Look, there's a café. Can I buy you a coffee—or better yet, a nice relaxing glass of wine?") You may need to separate from the host for an hour or two. Otherwise the Let's Go energy might propel you into a "Let's go home!" frame of mind.

3. THE TOO-CLOSE HOST

There are some hosts who are so excited to see you, and so happy to have you in their home, that they will follow you around every second you are there, practically into the bathroom, trying to be helpful. Unfortunately, there are times you just want to be left alone for a second. The Too-Close Host may be a little lonely, or just have a different sense of personal space. Anyway, she means well.

Handling Instructions

Here are some tricks to put a little distance between you and the Too-Close Host:

· Make a phone call.

· Offer to go out for milk or a newspaper.

· Go to the bathroom. (And shut the door.)

· When your host knocks on the door of your room, be "getting dressed."

4. THE GHOST HOST

On the other hand, I talked to someone who once went to visit a friend in Maine for four days and the host disappeared, leaving the guest alone, without a car or much to eat—for eight hours!

Staying Over

Another person recounted a horrifying tale of being left at home with the host's kids, without forewarning or any knowledge of the host's whereabouts. The missing host returned two hours later, making a vague reference to "stopping off to see some friends."

Handling Instructions

First, you must ascertain if the host is really gone (and not just in the garage or out in the yard). If it is clear there has been no emergency, and it has been over an hour, you may officially consider him a Ghost Host. Besides feeling totally free to raid the refrigerator and/or bar, you should phone any other acquaintances in the same geographical area and get them to come pick you up. Go do something fun (if there are no kids to mind). Leave the host a note or a message on his cell. Later, when the visit is over and you are back home, you might try asking the Ghost Host what made him disappear like that. There is probably an explanation, if not an excuse.

5. THE BOASTFUL HOST

The Boastful Host will tell you (and tell you, and tell you) that his city/favorite restaurant/neighborhood is the best to be experienced in all the world. The Boastful Host challenges you to deny that everything you see and hear is the best of its kind.

Handling Instructions

There is only one thing to do: Agree with the host that his town, his restaurant, his neighborhood, *is* in fact the best in the world. In other words, humor the Boastful Host. You can boast to your friends at home later on that you are the best houseguest in the world!

6. THE HARRIED HOST

The Harried Host opens the door with a wild look on her face. "All hell's broken out at the office," she might say. "And I just found

187

out we have termites, and my husband is stuck at the airport! But welcome! Please come on in." The Harried Host is under a lot more pressure than she was when she invited you.

Handling Instructions

As soon as you have diagnosed the Harried Host, get out of her way. Stick to your own quarters as much as possible. Offer to take her out for drinks or dessert. Put any requests or expectations you had for the weekend on the back burner.

7. THE RESENTFUL HOST

You can end up with a Resentful Host if 1) you are visiting a couple and one of them doesn't want you there or 2) your host changed his mind somewhere along the way and, while he was perfectly lovely about inviting you, he now seems to be regretting his decision—for what reason you really can't tell.

Handling Instructions

Don't feel guilty. Don't let the Resentful Host get to you. He is behaving badly, not you. However, your best bet is to flatter, praise, and otherwise soothe the Resentful Host. You may be able to soften him up. It's always advisable to treat fear (which is the basis of all resentments) with love, if you can.

8. THE MORE-THE-MERRIER HOST

This is the kind of host who, without giving a guest fair warning or any choice about it, invites other people to stay for the same weekend—sometimes a *lot* of other people. You might find out about it only when you've already arrived.

Handling Instructions

Get into the spirit of this host. Unless one of the other guests is someone with whom you are feuding, try to loosen up and go with it. Have fun. The More-the-Merrier Host is a generous person.

The weekend may be chaotic, and you may not have the quality time with the host you were hoping for, but there is nothing to do but try to get into the group experience.

9. THE MOROSE HOST

You arrive and there is something terribly wrong with the mood of the house. The host is moping around, covered in gloom. He is not himself, he is hardly smiling at all, and when you ask him what is wrong he just shrugs.

Handling Instructions

After your initial efforts, don't try too much to cheer up the Morose Host. When in Rome, do as the Romans do; when in gloom... Like the Grumpy Guest, the Morose Host is enjoying his moroseness on some level. You can't jolly him out of it. And remember, the best guests go with the flow.

10. THE TASKMASTER HOST

Some hosts—especially if they live in the country—really do put you to work as soon as you take your coat off. They often are so used to being active, and there is so much to do, that they don't realize you might not be into it.

Handling Instructions

Be very, very slow at any job you are given. (As with a factory slowdown, the host may get the message that you are rebelling). Also, tempt the host into nonwork mode. Give her a backrub, make her a drink, tell her *she* needs to take a break.

Always remember what a special treat and honor it is to be invited to stay at a friend's home. It is often an important step in relationships. You can learn as much about someone by being in her home for one weekend as you could during a dozen restaurant excursions.

CHAPTER 8

The Social Sophisticate

DEALING WITH UNEXPECTED SITUATIONS

I know of one hostess who, after stepping out for some groceries, came home to find that her houseguest had dropped dead in the middle of the living room (which I must say was very bad manners on his part). I heard another story about a woman who, having received permission from the host to bring her poodle on a weekend visit, ended up having to sleep for both nights on the kitchen floor with her hand on the dog to keep him quiet. I have heard cautionary tales involving stoves bursting into flames, guests bursting into tears, and too-tight cocktail dresses bursting at the seams.

Whether you are hosting or guesting, you can plan everything perfectly, behave impeccably, and still have your weekend or evening turn into a disaster, due to the unpredictable nature of people and of life itself. Many of us who have had social situations blow up in our faces think: *Why should I put myself in harm's way again? Isn't it just safer to stay home alone?*

No. You can never control the universe, and like everything else in life, at-home entertaining can be a messy thing. But that's no reason not to do it. Keep in mind that each time you get through a difficult social situation, you become a more proficient, wiser guest or host. Plus, you may end up with a really good story to entertain your friends with for years to come!

Managing Unforeseen Circumstances

Life is apt to throw you a few curveballs. (In fact, life is made up of mostly curveballs). You can prepare for weeks and still, the day of the party the electricity can go out, the guests can fail to show up, or you can sprain your wrist while putting the turkey in the oven. Fate may just decide to step in and change your perfect plans.

Navigating surprises in the social realm often requires more effort and finesse than other areas in life. There will be those times when you will need to rise to the occasion—to take control of a bad situation and fix it—and other times when the solution is in doing nothing, in just letting things play out. Consider the following social quandaries caused by unforeseen events:

Chicken Pox Pie

Penny had been planning a dinner for weeks. There were ten guests coming, some traveling from quite a distance. Five hours before the party was to begin, Penny's twelve-year-old daughter came down with the chicken pox. Although the doctor assured her that there was minimal risk to any guest (even those who had not had the disease in childhood), as the patient would be confined to her upstairs bedroom, Penny was still torn. She had already bought the steaks and shrimp. She was loath to cancel the party, but didn't she have a responsibility to inform her guests?

Penny did the right thing: She called everyone up (thank god for cell phones), told them her daughter had chicken pox, and assured them that she would be kept in her bedroom but that any guests' reluctance to come would be completely understood. She did lose three guests, who told her they were not at all confident that they had had chicken pox as children. (Chicken pox can be dreadful if you get it as an adult.)

Moral: It is always advisable, when faced with this kind of choice, to put your guests' needs and concerns before your own. They will appreciate it; full disclosure is usually good for your relationship with friends. Moreover, had her guests not been apprised, Penny might have had a mid-party freak-out on her hands.

Note: If Penny or a family member had had a common variety of cold or flu, she would not have had an obligation to inform the guests, unless any were old or infirm.

Alarming Houseguest

It was 2:00 in the morning and Herman was starving. He decided that he would sneak down to his host's kitchen and get something to eat. He assumed that no one would be the wiser, as long as he was quiet. He found some apple pie in the refrigerator, but as he was cutting himself a slice, he couldn't help thinking how much better it would be if it were heated up—and after all it would only take a second.

How could he have known that the toaster oven would start smoldering? When the piercing alarm went off, Herman quickly located the smoke detector but could not figure out how to turn it off. The host finally emerged, bleary-eyed and none too thrilled at having been awakened. The next day, Herman got up early, cleaned the toaster oven and the kitchen, and took the host out to a nice brunch.

Moral: It's never a good idea to cook—or build a fire, or light a gas heater—in someone else's house when the host is not around, unless he knows you are doing it. Raid the fridge if you dare, but stick to cold leftovers.

The Guest Who Would Be Host

Charles was invited to a dinner party; in fact, he was the guest of honor. The other guests were arriving at 8:00, but Charles had arrived for an early drink, as requested. At 7:30, the hosts got an emergency phone call. A close relative had suddenly been taken to the hospital; both hosts rushed out the door.

Charles didn't miss a beat. He went into the kitchen, finished preparing the dinner, and graciously greeted the other guests. The whole party was, of course, concerned for the hosts, but Charles knew that they were the kind of people who believe fervently that the dinner party must go on. (I think Charles even gave himself a toast.)

Moral: Always be prepared to help out. Like the salamander who can regrow a limb, when the party loses an important part, all guests should be ready to slip into other roles for the good of the evening. Think of all social situations as team efforts.

Non-Meshable Guests

To accommodate friends coming to their city for a college reunion, Ellen and John had invited several people to stay at their house for the weekend. Unfortunately, John failed to mention to Ellen that at the last minute he had invited Brett, who had long ago had a terrible falling out with another one of their houseguests, Danielle. Danielle and Brett had not spoken to each other for four years (though no one knew why).

They all gathered on the patio on the first evening. The entire group held their breaths as Brett and Danielle spotted one another. Neither of them had known the other was coming.

John took Brett aside under the pretext of fetching him a drink, and apologized for not forewarning him; Ellen did the same thing for Danielle. Much to everyone's immense relief, the two guests themselves became the heroes of the story; they took the high road and behaved civilly toward each other. After a while they didn't have to pretend; the two quarreling college buddies kissed and made up.

Moral: Never underestimate the power of a social event to bring out people's best selves.

Surprise!

It is almost impossible to succeed in pulling off the surprise part of a surprise party, which is why the friends and business acquaintances of Billy were so smug about having done it. When they ambushed him in the dark in his apartment at 9:00 on a Saturday night, they knew he would never know what hit him. Unfortunately neither did his date, who was, alas, the wife of one of the planners.

Moral: Surprise parties are difficult to plan and can cause more stress than enjoyment in the end. The object of the surprise often either has to fake being surprised, which no one should have to do (especially if it is his birthday), or is made uncomfortable by being caught off guard and unprepared for socializing. And any guest arriving late is terrified or guilt-ridden about spoiling the surprise.

What to Do About Drunkenness or Violent Arguments

Now and then, in the middle of a perfectly serene evening, a social storm suddenly whips up out of nowhere. Someone pushes someone else's button, or crosses a line. To wit, sometimes one of the guests—or the host herself—goes haywire.

Are You a Good Drunk or a Bad Drunk?

It's a terrible cliché, but one of the main causes of a guest disturbing the peace and tranquility of your party is bad drinking. Not just heavy drinking, but *bad* drinking.

Getting drunk is never anything to aspire to, but there are people who can drink quite a bit and still be socially viable. In other words, they don't become maudlin, or belligerent, or sloppy, or destructive, or mean, or lewd, or ugly in any way. These are "good" drunks. A "bad" drunk, on the other hand, is not someone you want at your table. A bad drunk can really ruin your party. A bad drunk can knock over chairs and gravy boats and say things like, "Why the hell aren't you married? I'd have *shex* with you in a *heartsbeat.*"

Once you realize you have a bad drunk on your hands, there is little sense in trying to make the drunk stop drinking. (Though one trick that works somewhat is to keep filling his glass with mostly water. But you are fighting a losing battle.)

Most of us know this already, but it bears repeating: You should not try to argue with a drunk. You need to humor him—and get him out of your apartment or house as soon as possible, as long as you are absolutely certain he will not be driving. Smile benignly and nod when he speaks and then immediately turn to engage one of the other guests, who will be as interested as you are in shutting the drunk up.

The Pitfalls of Politics

It can happen in an instant: One minute you are discussing how hot the weather was that day and the next you've got two people yelling across the table at each other, calling each other names. Suddenly you remember that Fred is, in fact, a staunch Republican and all the other guests are Democrats.

There is hardly any way to avoid the subject of politics these days. How can intelligent people gathered together for conversation totally avoid touching on the environment, foreign policy, the price of oil, health care? A lively political discussion can be invigorating, as long as everyone present is either very level-headed or more or less on the same side (although sometimes even people who are on your side can be so fanatical that their tirades aren't fun to listen to). However, once you realize someone has reached a boiling point and is about to blow, you must help put a stop to the discussion for the good of the party.

Whether you are the host or a guest, try to diffuse the situation and change the subject, using a line like one of the following:

- "Well, I don't know about that, but there's one thing I do know about: I'm hungry! Will someone pass the turkey? Jill, how did you make this gravy? It's delicious!"

- "Listen to us arguing! No wonder my mother always told me never to talk politics at a party! Why don't we talk about sex instead!"

- (Jokingly) "Well, I guess you guys better either talk about something else or step outside! By the way, is it still raining out there?"

- "Let us drink to a difference of opinion, to good company, and—most of all—to our host! This dinner is fabulous."

Is There a Therapist in the House?

Most of us have been present at a party or a dinner when parents totally lose it with their kids or a couple has a major fight. This can be incredibly uncomfortable for the bystanders, whether the squabblers are guests or hosts. No one ever knows whether to try to step in and mediate, leave, or what. Sometimes your impulse is to just cover your ears and hide under the table as if there were bombs going off; other times you can be tempted to join in the yelling yourselves to try to make the fighting stop. Of course, neither reaction is appropriate or constructive.

If the violent argument is occurring in someone else's home, the best thing to do (if you can manage it) is to breathe deeply and pretend it is not happening. I'm sure there are many therapists who will tell you this is an unhealthy form of denial, but I believe it is socially expedient to avoid participation in fights that do not concern you. Of course, if it comes to blows, that is another matter (or if there is a good reason to believe you really can help the situation—for instance, if they are fighting over you). The idea behind this course of inaction is to try to get the screamers to realize that there is a party still going on, and that their combative behavior is unacceptable. If the fight takes place in your home, distraction—an aunt's favorite tool for handling misbehaving children—is the best remedy. ("Anyone ready for dessert?")

Always give people the benefit of the doubt. Your furious friends might be having a bad night, so you should forgive an occasional outburst. But if, after three or four times of having dinner at their house, it's still a war zone, stop going there—at least for a while. It defeats all purposes of socializing (that is, to have fun and to further friendship) if you are forced to witness interpersonal carnage.

Triangulation and Other Psychological Minefields

Triangulation is the process whereby one person who has an issue with someone uses a third party to validate his feelings. This is also known as getting sucked into a fight.

In its extreme form, triangulation can make you feel as if you are trapped in a scene from *Who's Afraid of Virginia Woolf?*, a well-known play in which an unsuspecting couple is drawn into drunken, hellish relationship "games." Triangulation doesn't always manifest in an actual argument; it can be a much more subtle thing than that. But it's always dicey for the third person.

Triangles in social life are uncomfortable, unwieldy structures. There is a good reason they call it a third wheel—it's uneven. From the time we are little, three friends is always harder to negotiate than two. Within the threesome, the balance is continuously shifting between one pair and another. One person always feels left out, even if only slightly.

Usually the triangulators are a couple who know each other well—either a married couple or two old friends (and you are the newcomer to the trio). It happens this way:

You are all sitting around having a perfectly nice time, when one of the couple says something like:

· "We've been trying to settle an argument..."
· "Wait: let's get a fresh opinion on this now that *you* are here."
· "My idiotic husband here doesn't think we should repair the roof. Don't you think it looks like it's going to fall down?"

Oops. You've just stepped on a mine, or you are about to. Do you hear the warning bells going off? Often this happens when

199

there are only three of you in the room, but not always. Two people can use a whole table of people to triangulate; sometimes the hosts are in bickering mode and try to drag all the guests in.

At the first sign that you have entered an area that is a trouble spot for this couple, back away, as gingerly as you can, but immediately. If you have a conviction you might be able to help, and they actively solicit your advice, proceed with extreme caution. But if you have even the slightest doubt of your territory, plead the fifth or leave the house to go get the paper.

We are only human, and you can find yourself sucked in before you know it. Suddenly you can feel the tension building, and you are not even sure how it happened. If you are not able to sidestep a triangulation issue, then you must try to mediate, to stay as much as you can in the middle. Take both sides; see both points of view. But try very hard not to be a part of a ganging-up situation. You can always joke, "Hey you guys, don't drag me into this! I am not a licensed therapist."

Sometimes, of course, the minefield you find yourself in has nothing to do with triangulation. You might casually mention something you had no idea was a secret, inadvertently causing trouble. You might hurt someone's feelings by accident, having no idea that she was super-sensitive in a particular area. You might be unaware that one of the guests you've invited to your cocktail party is about to have a breakdown, in which he sits alone in a corner for two hours and then suddenly stands up and throws a glass across the room shouting, "I just can't take my life anymore!" The only way to deal with these unexpected explosions or difficulties is with as much compassion, humor, and grace—and respect for the other guests present—as possible. Try not to be judgmental, and try not to get drawn into other people's drama.

Emergency Socializing, or the Guest Who Came in from the Cold

It was going to be a wonderful concert. It was, after all, nothing less than Pavarotti in Central Park, and our picnic blanket was situated a mere fifty feet from the stage, promising an evening of sheer heaven. Luciano and his ubiquitous white handkerchief appeared, and we all breathed a blissful sigh as he started singing. After only two songs, however, the skies opened up and there was a violent, torrential downpour.

Anyone who lives in Manhattan knows that Central Park can flood very quickly. There we were—along with 100,000 other people—desperate to make our way out of the park, wading through mud and water that was, in some places, up to our knees. By the time we emerged onto the street, we were utterly drenched.

Then a couple who was part of our group did the most wonderful, generous, and hospitable thing: They invited all seven of us up to their nearby apartment, where they provided us all with luxuriously dry bathrobes and sweats and big snifters of bourbon. They put our clothes in the dryer and ordered up pizza.

There is something special that happens when you go from physically uncomfortable conditions—especially if you have been out of doors, and the foul weather took you by surprise—directly into the warmth and security of someone's home. The affection and gratitude a guest normally feels is multiplied tenfold. In addition, the emergency hosts can't be expected to have prepared in any way (not even a little), so anything they manage to produce for the guests seems like a miracle of hospitality. The guests feel as though there were never hosts so brilliant—whether it is towels, beer and potato chips, or merely spring water that have instantaneously materialized.

That night, I became best friends with almost everyone in that apartment. (I even fell in love with one of them. But that's another story.) We felt we were all in some fairy tale cabin, safe from the storm; we sang, we told stories about our childhoods. What a shame you can't prearrange these socially advantageous kinds of disasters!

Our hosts that night did everything right—they acted generously, without hesitation—and somehow we never got the impression we were putting them out at all. We ended up feeling that we actually had a better time than if we had gotten to hear the whole concert.

Calamities and mishaps of one kind or another can bring people closer. I became better friends with neighbors I hunkered down with during the East Coast blackout in the summer of 2003. I have made connections with people because we were stranded on a broken-down subway train or waiting at an airport for a plane that seemed to never come. I have talked to many people who have bonded with others because they were stuck in an elevator or they survived a really bad disaster together.

If you have an opportunity to give someone safe haven during some type of emergency, whether natural or man-made, or just help to rescue a social event that has gone awry for some reason, by all means do it. It's a wonderful way to reach out to people and will make you feel great. Order takeout, eat whatever is in the fridge, or send a guest who volunteers out for supplies. Relish the fact that you have company during a stressful situation; see where the evening takes you. It is good for your hosting muscles to practice just winging it and not worrying whether there are dishes in the sink or newspapers on the floor.

Whatever the situation, make your connections with people a priority. Never cancel any social event just because you hit a snag.

I once had a birthday party planned and at the last minute I found I was sequestered on a jury. I refused to cancel my party, so the court let me host it—with two armed guards by my side. Far from it being a bust, it ended up being one of my most memorable parties ever!

CHAPTER 9

Socializing with Neighbors, Family, and Friends from Your Past

There are always going to be people in your life with whom you have a compartmentalized form of intimacy. It may be your next-door neighbor who sees you getting the morning paper in your pajamas and who knows how you talk to your children when you think no one is listening. It may be a sibling who lives far away, a childhood friend who knew you way back when, or a buddy at work who you see every day, but only during working hours. These are people who know a particular side of you extremely well—better than almost anyone—but who do not know the whole you. And yet they have a strong, sometimes permanent, presence in your life.

The guidelines for playdates and/or sleepovers with neighbors, family, or childhood friends are a little different from the normal guidelines. Whereas ordinarily you are socializing with the goal of getting to know people better—and the intimacy level grows gradually and organically from that process—the challenge here is that these people already know you well (or they think they do). These are folks who may take you for granted (and vice versa) and sometimes even take advantage of you. Although many of them are not necessarily people you would have chosen to be in your inner circle, the stakes are nevertheless often high. With familiarity born of proximity or blood or your early history comes an increased need for one of the most important elements of relationships: *boundaries.*

Proximity Warnings: Survival Techniques for Socializing with Your Neighbors

We've all heard of neighbors from hell: They're the ones who call the police when your dog is barking or who keep you up all night with loud music. And some of you may have experienced overly needy neighbors, the ones who will continually ask you to sign for their packages, sit with their kids, and lend them things. Those two types of neighbors present difficult but clear-cut problems.

But what about neighbors who seem nice and are eager to become friends with you—who want to go shopping, play golf, go to the movies, and have dinners together? Shouldn't you just say "Come on in; my house is yours"? Isn't that the neighborly thing to do?

They say you can't choose your family, but you also can't always choose your neighbors, which is why you have to be extremely careful in deciding whether or not to socialize with them. Some readers may be surprised at my advising caution—especially as this whole book is about inviting people over to your house. But it's important to be sure you are choosing the friends you invite into your life and not merely socializing with them because they happen to live next door.

Indeed, many people have a totally closed-door policy when it comes to neighbors, because they realize that once they start having them over, they will never be able to *stop* having them over, even if they realize the neighbors are not as much fun as they thought they might be. It is very hard to define boundaries, not to mention protect your privacy, with people who are almost literally in your backyard. (This is, of course, why fences were invented. They are really more of a psychological boundary than a physical one.)

It's difficult to go back to being just "Hello, how are you?" neighbors once you have asked them over and let them into your life. Therefore, you have to be almost positive that you really, really like these people before you cross the line from neighbor to friend. Think carefully before you invite your neighbor over to supper; you have to have a real sense that you are not going to regret it. Living close to one another can produce a sort of fake intimacy, which can be confusing.

Socializing with neighbors is one of those things that is somewhat different for people in urban areas than for people in suburban areas. In the suburbs or a small town, your kids probably play with the neighbor's kids, and therefore you may naturally do a certain amount of socializing with the parents—though you can still limit socializing with them when the kids are not involved. In a city like New York, people's need for privacy is greatly increased, and so is the sense of boundaries. This is why New Yorkers rarely become good friends with their next-door neighbors. When you come home to an apartment in a crowded city, you really need to have it be your own protected space.

Your neighbors are likely to have the same reticence you do about pursuing a friendship. They will probably understand as much as you that there is a big difference between the neighborhood socializing that is done across the hedge or in the lobby of your building and becoming best friends. Everyone realizes the danger; no one has the time and energy to have to be dodging a neighbor—waiting for another elevator so you don't have to talk to them, or stealing out in the dark to get the paper. It's much safer to protect yourself.

Open Heart, Closed Door

When delineating your boundaries, you should never behave in a cold or standoffish manner. You should always be neighborly, and always be friendly. Smile, say hello, chat about things that concern the neighborhood, the building, the district you live in, the sewer system, and so on. But unless you are sure you want to cross into friend territory (always remembering you can't cross back), don't discuss your relationships or family, other than in a very general way. In other words, say, "We're going to Rochester for the holidays," but do not say, "I had a big fight with my husband over going home to Rochester for the holidays."

The trick is to be as friendly, kind, and considerate as possible to your neighbors while avoiding any infringement into the rest of your life.

Of course you should never shy away from helping out a neighbor, especially if it's someone who is old or sick or otherwise in need.

Open Heart, Open Door

If you should decide to go from friendly neighbor to friend, make the transition slowly. Have her over for a quick cup of coffee at first. Don't immediately start having dinners with her—unless, of course, you are lucky enough to find yourself with a neighbor who you recognize right away as a kindred spirit. In that case, you can certainly ignore all this conservative advice; you will enjoy a wonderful blessing, a neighbor who is also a friend. But this is rare.

The only time I experienced this kind of instant connection with neighbors was with a very cool couple who lived across the hall from me, Mitch and Allen. They knocked on my door one day to commiserate about a neurotic neighbor who had complained to the police about their two kids crying. (Mitch and Allen's twins were four, and naturally four-year-olds will cry sometimes. The dog upstairs was much louder.) I soon found out that Allen, like me, made fantastic martinis, and in no time at all the family became my dream neighbors; we could count on each other and we also had great fun.

But that doesn't mean we didn't maintain firm boundaries. Sometimes they would ask me in for a drink on the spur of the moment, but mostly we still made plans by phone—even though they were mere feet away from me. We all respected the fact that, because we lived across the hall from each other (and we weren't in a college dorm), we needed space and privacy. It is essential to adhere to strict boundaries when you are in such close proximity to each other.

Social Melting Pot:
Mixing Business and Pleasure

Without a doubt, friendships forged from working together for a long time can be some of the best friendships you ever have, but making friends with colleagues from work is similar in some ways to making friends with neighbors. You are going to see these people every day no matter what happens.

In addition, with coworkers, you have the added issue of the potential disintegration of the important barrier between your personal and your work life. Be sure you want that protective barrier to come down. You have got to really trust that this work friend has the same sense of boundaries that you do; you don't want to walk into the office and hear him telling your other colleagues about the poster of Paris Hilton he's seen in your bathroom at home.

Taking the relationship from the workplace to your personal life is as risky as it is rewarding. As with neighbors, you risk unpleasantness if it doesn't work out for some reason, and you have the additional danger of it being involved with your livelihood. It is for this reason that many people adopt a sort of "semi-friend" position with work friends. You socialize, but only within very specific parameters: You will go out for lunch, drinks, or dinner after work, but not on weekends, and you make certain there is no crossover with your other friends. If you keep your work and personal worlds separated, you feel a little safer. It can still be a very fulfilling relationship. Often you can have a sort of "therapy-esque" back-and-forth with the work friend; because this friend is never going to meet your wife or your other friends, you can talk about home life problems—as long as you trust the coworker not to share them at the board meeting.

Note: It is almost impossible to make friends with a coworker after one of you has left the company. If you never crossed over into friendship while you were working together, it's probably too late—too after-the-fact—to become friends after one of you has changed jobs.

Parents Are from Pluto

You may be one of those people whose parents are their best friends. For you, there may be no generation gap, no communication gap, no pesky leftover childhood issues. And let me say that if my own mother and father are reading this: I'm one of those people, Mom and Dad! Now will you two please go back to your crossword puzzle so I can tell the truth to my readers?

Many of us have a sense of foreboding about the houseguest visit from parents. It's really a strange kind of discomfort, considering they are the people who raised us, the people who probably loved us unconditionally. Why should the most intimate relationship of our lives take so much effort? Didn't we live in the same house with parents for eighteen years or so?

Keep in mind that parents are usually uncomfortable not only with the fact that their child has become an adult, but with the reversal of roles; your being host and their being guests can be stressful for them. When the parents come to stay with you, they are on your turf and may suffer from Topsy-Turvy Syndrome. They are supposed to be in charge, not you. They are supposed to be feeding and housing you, not the other way around. All together, it can make them feel like aliens.

Herein lies the secret trick when socializing with parents. We have all heard about men being from Mars and women from Venus;

well, just think of your parents as being from Pluto. Everything will be hunky-dory if you simply pretend they are visiting from another planet. If you think of them as coming from a whole different universe, you will be much more patient with their needs and habits.

After all, if someone from Pluto came to visit you, wouldn't you be compassionate about how alien they feel? Wouldn't you assume a certain amount of frustration in your communications, and be more patient with the aliens? Wouldn't you try hard to find out what food they like, how to make them more comfortable, so they have a favorable impression of our planet?

Of course, from the parents' point of view it is you who are from another planet. Much of the conflict with parents and their adult children stems from the fact that the adult child has become a whole new person. This is why parents are more comfortable when you visit them; you are more likely to temporarily revert to your childhood self.

Negotiation before the visit is extremely important (see page 143); all planning about the schedule, the menu, the sleeping arrangements, and everything else should be handled in detail before any parental houseguesting. Give the Plutonians every possible comfort. Don't lecture them or try to change them while they are in your house; wait until you go to visit them.

Acts of God: The In-Laws and Other Inherited Relationships

Much easier in some ways are the relationships you inherit—people to whom you are connected whether you like it or not, but with whom you are more or less starting from scratch. There are a lot of people—in-laws, wives of friends, your spouse's college roommate—who are simply in your life, and you have to make the best of it. Some will become your genuine friends; others never will. But for the sake of the person who connects you to them, you act as if they are friends. Unlike neighbors and members of your own family, you can get to know these folks gradually. (I have heard a few stories of people who even became good friends with their in-laws. It can happen.)

It's very odd, these people who are so tightly tied to you and are in many cases your intimates, but whom you did not choose. The best thing is to try to see them as presents to your life.

On the other hand, I talked to one woman who has a cousin by marriage who is a paranoid schizophrenic, and every time he comes to visit it is a nightmare. There are also friends who marry people with whom we have trouble getting along. There is only one thing I can say about these kinds of inherited relationships; in the words of Tim Gunn: "Make it work, people."

How to Truly Enjoy the Old Friend without Regressing

Old friends are to be cherished. They sustain us, nurture us, validate us; in a lot of ways, they define who we are. But sometimes when that old college friend you haven't seen for eight years comes to visit, you may find yourself feeling confused. On a visceral level, you each expect the other to be the same person you remember. But people can change a lot in eight years. You may find yourself having to make an effort to assert yourself, stay true to the person you are now, and not regress to a former version of yourself. Maybe you both used to drink ten beers at a sitting, and he still does but you don't. Maybe you used to be the person everyone teased but you have since changed. Maybe he's found God and you've lost God. Maybe you've been in therapy for ten years and she hasn't. If you have been in constant touch with each other, your reentry into the friendship may be seamless; if not, you may have to go through a "synching up" period.

Friend Synch

On the first day of your visit from (or to) a very old friend, you have to catch up to each other (as well as with each other), get back in tune with each other, and adjust your past perceptions to match your present ones—as well as reconnect to the great friendship energy you shared before. There is often a period of awkwardness, even discomfort, while the synching up is happening. You may feel weird or sad. In almost all cases, when you get past this initial period, it is a great visit. So you just have to take a deep breath, trust the connection, and wait for it to kick in. This "synching up" period will last anywhere from an hour to a day.

Resuscitating Stagnant Friendships

A lot of people think I am kind of crazy the way I won't let friends disappear. I can't help it; when I meet someone I love, it is like a diamond I have in my hands and I don't like to see it slip away. (When friends compliment me on how well I keep in touch with people, I always joke, "Once you are my friend I hold on like Grim Death." And many people look at me nervously.)

Even if you are not an old friend fanatic like me, it might be worth it to do what I occasionally do: I flip through my phone book, or scroll through my e-mail address book. There are usually names of people there I have lost touch with, for no good reason other than life got busy or I called them and they never called me back. Shoot them a quick e-mail. E-mail is great for saying hello after a long time hass passed. It may feel as if you are trying to reach across a great expanse of space and time, but all you have to write is, "For some reason I was thinking about you today. How are you?"

CHAPTER 10

The Joys and Challenges of Serial Socializing

People need routine. From monthly book clubs to yearly visits with friends, regular socializing provides us with social routine. It's like a security blanket in the ever-changing configurations of our lives. Even though these types of activities do not, by any means, make up our whole social lives, we like to be able to count on the structure of regular social enjoyments. The familiarity of the people and the ongoing nature of the activity are satisfying, reassuring, and relaxing to us.

Serial socializing is also one of the ways in which we lay the groundwork for more intimacy in our lives. We can deepen connections with people by seeing them over and over. After a while, these people will know our personal histories, so we can keep getting to more nuanced levels with each other, as the years of sharing the experience accrue.

This kind of socializing is also a big bang for your buck. One of the greatest benefits of serial socializing is that once you get it going, it is like a perpetual motion machine—it just happens without your having to do much (besides show up). Whether it's every third Tuesday of the month or a semi-regular evening that takes a little more scheduling (thank god for e-mail), you never have to start from scratch.

Book Clubs, Poker Night, and Other Regular Groups

For twenty years, I have held sacrosanct my women's poker night. I never cancel poker, even if I have to turn down a ticket to the theater or some other tasty social offering. My poker night is usually great fun—but not always. There are some nights I wonder: *Why am I still doing this? Is this just a part of my past I can't let go of?*

The truth is, it is not just the fun of playing the game (which I do love), but the time spent, the years of the group's history, that make it so rewarding. When you have a regular social thing for twenty years, it is like creating a little family together. And as in any close group, you will hit relationship bumps in the road, because that is part of intimacy. My poker group is a little bit family, a little bit group therapy, a little bit "girls' night out," and a little bit Vegas.

There are some clubs that are purely social. I know of many breakfast clubs where people meet at a coffee shop, read the newspapers, and discuss the day's events before heading off to work. It's a very grounding way to start the day. Lunch and dinner groups are a popular form of serial socializing. Some of them may be industry related, but they are still primarily social clubs. For example, I know of many writers' and publishing lunch groups, but they are not usually lunching with the people they do business with. There are groups that serve more of a support/social purpose: divorced women groups, mothers' groups, single women groups, widowed women groups. Then there are groups organized around an activity (book clubs, card-playing clubs, movie groups, theater clubs) and team-oriented groups (Monday night football, bowling night, Sunday soccer, etc.).

Keep in mind that your club doesn't have to be more than a group of two. Many friends have a set weekly drink or coffee date that they look forward to and depend on.

Guys' Night/Girls' Night Out

Years ago, the "guys' night out" cliché had a bad rap, yet it was really a model for a fine idea. When it became girls' night out, the concept became acceptable again. Men's groups tend to be more game oriented: poker night, sports night. Men are more likely to get together and "do" rather than talk, which of course is just as deeply rewarding and enriching. Women tend to participate in regular group social activities more than men. It is mostly women who have book clubs and dinner clubs; they also often have regular game nights. I have heard a lot from suburban women about a revolving game called Bunco (a game involving dice, scorecards, and multiple tables of players) that sounds like just an excuse for the women of the neighborhood to get together, eat and drink, and giggle. (The best reasons for getting together I can think of!)

Social Club Process
Scheduling
If the date is not part of the club's set-up (as in, the club always meets on the first Wednesday of the month), scheduling can be challenging, depending on the number of members and the level of their commitment to the club. They best way to operate is for

whoever is hosting to be in charge of sending out a group e-mail to all of the members, offering several choices of dates. The date that suits the most people wins. There should be no bickering back and forth about this; the host should be in charge here.

It's not always easy. Trying to schedule eight busy women for a poker game or ten working mothers for a dinner can be time-consuming. Usually the hosting responsibility is shared by the members of the group, although often some people will host more than others because they have a better home for it (lots of space for entertaining, a big card table, or a location central to everyone in the group).

Membership Maintenance

How membership is decided is specific to each group. However, clubs usually start with a core of people who are the ones who founded it, and then they decide how new people will be invited in. Some groups are very loose and open to any friend of a member; other groups have a screening process by which they decide on new members, either by vote or by caucus. This may sound overly exclusive, but if it is a small group, a new person can destroy the dynamic.

I heard a story of one book club that had been going on for about six years. One February, one of the members brought a guest. The guest started coming regularly, but every time she came she monopolized the conversation and seemed to hate every book that was chosen. Soon the meetings became so unappetizing for other club members that the club started losing people. So the four founders of the group made a drastic move. They disbanded the book club—supposedly for good, but in actuality for a period of six months. Then they surreptitiously started it up again without informing either the member who had hosted the "difficult guest" or the difficult guest herself.

Socially Sealed?

Sometimes your serial socializing is done with friends in the neighborhood who you already see several times a week. But often serial socializing activities are completely separate from the rest of your life. There is something very relaxing about a totally separate social realm. On the other hand, sometimes it starts out as totally compartmentalized but you find that you like someone so much you decide to start seeing them on the side. If you do this, for a while you will only talk about the group, until gradually your friendship develops and overlaps into the rest of your life.

A Little Bit of Heaven: Revolving Dinner Parties

In my opinion, revolving dinners are the Xanadu not just of socializing, but of life. In some dinner groups everyone goes to a restaurant (these are often groups who are interested in trying out new places), but for me the ultimate is the at-home revolving dinner party. This can be one of the most rewarding social practices you can have, providing it's with people who really feed your heart and soul. If it's just your weekly dinner with the people next door because you are too lazy to set out in the world and make new friends, it won't be the paradise it can be.

The best groups have from five to eight members. Each member in the revolving dinner group takes turns hosting the group at his home. You may have a dinner group that is organized around a special kind of cuisine, so that each time a person hosts a dinner, it is to try another kind of truffle. (But the evening is never about the food; the food is just the accoutrement.) Your dinner group may be organized—or galvanized—around listening to a type of music or watching a particular genre of old movie. (Sorry, but I frown on eating *during* the movie.)

You may also choose to have progressive dinner parties, which are great for socializing with neighbors. You start at one person's house for drinks, move on to someone else's for the first course, and so on, until you run out of homes (and food).

Revolving dinner parties combine the warm intimacy of friends eating together at home with the dependable nature of serial socializing. Let's say you have found a group of five or six of you who, when you meet, feel completely sparked—energized and alive. Your minds respond to one another, your differences are interesting, even enlightening. You find a common taste in food or music; you find you love to talk about the same movies. You learn more every time you get together, and yet it feels like coming home. You decide to have dinners once a month, without fail. Your life becomes brighter, you feel more connected. A good dinner group is like a long love affair.

Field Tripping: Sharing Trivial (or Not So Trivial) Pursuits

Once you realize you have a friend (or a group of acquaintances) who shares an interest like flea marketing or jewelry making, planning outings around that interest is a great way to get motivated about getting together. In addition, you build a relationship the way people do when they work together, based on being engaged in something you both like. It's something to focus on, to always have more conversations about. It can be the best kind of sharing.

Part of the reason people are not motivated to call each other and be proactive about doing things is that it sometimes seems too forward to just call someone out of the blue and say, "I want to see you, let's have dinner." It's almost too datelike. But if you call and say, "Hey, I know you are into ballet and there is a ballet troupe in town..." it seems completely appropriate.

This kind of serial socializing is different from the book club kind of socializing, because while you hope to arrange these "field trips" frequently and regularly, you can't count on it the same way. Field tripping takes a bit more effort because your get-togethers are not automatically set for a regular time. However, if a group of you find you have a common interest—jogging, knitting, early American pottery—it is well worth it to get the group organized.

Creating Your Own Traditions: The Regularly Scheduled Visit

Every third weekend in May, according to one woman I interviewed, she and four other women who went to high school together leave their families and meet up at a cabin on a lake in Wisconsin. They began this tradition when the mother of one of the women died and the friends all wanted to show their support for her. They had so much fun, and felt they got so much out of the weekend, that they started doing it every year—as hard as it is to schedule.

Many people make a point of incorporating these kinds of visits into their lives. For many years, I went to Kentucky on the last weekend in October to see friends and go to the races at Keeneland (until these friends moved last year, alas). My sister has started coming to see me every May. I have other friends who always come for July Fourth. These kinds of set-in-stone house-guesting rituals give your life a shape; the visits are like wonderful islands of fun situated here and there in your calendar year. You can look forward to them and count on them, the way you might have counted on Christmas or Halloween when you were a kid.

The one proviso about these traditions is that, as important as it is to strive for longevity (because the older the tradition gets, the richer it can be), you have to be sure you are still reaping positive things from the visit. Sometimes it was a good idea when you started it, but for one or all of the participants, the meaning and fun has dissipated to the point where you are just going through the motions. Don't keep doing it only because you have been doing it. (You can always create a new tradition with someone new.) It can be hard to know how to break the pattern, to turn off the perpetual motion machine. It may take a couple of years to shake off the person who is still interested, or it may be mutual and easy.

However, don't let the regularly scheduled visit go by the wayside simply because it's become difficult to schedule. Make it a priority. These are the important things in life—more important than your dentist appointment, a home repair project, or even a work deadline (please don't tell my editor I said that).

Wet Towels and Dry Martinis: Traveling with Friends

Traveling with your friends is something to be entered into with extreme caution. It can be the most fun you ever have, but it also could break up a friendship. It's a very intense form of socializing. How many stories have we all heard about the trip that so-and-so went on with her very best friend in the world and afterward they didn't speak to each other for months?

You may be very fond of one another, you may be fine dinner companions, and even do well houseguesting at each of your homes (where at least someone is on familiar territory), but when you take it on the road, you are taking a chance. There is something about the stress of traveling, about all the choices you have to make regarding your comfort, which—combined with your separate agendas and desires for the trip (what to see, where to eat)—puts a great strain on a relationship. Add to that the subconscious fear everyone has about being stranded or away from home, and it may not be worth it.

Remember, traveling together is *not* a necessary step in your friendship-building process. At-home entertaining, yes; traveling together, no.

If you are not natural-born travel companions, communicate a lot beforehand. Don't assume anything. Talk a lot about all the details of the trip. When you are sharing a vacation house together, that is, a vacation house that does not belong to either of you but is a place you rent together for the summer, try to split everything down the middle. Believe it or not, I have heard shocking stories of people sharing a beach house for the weekend and getting to the grocery store where one of the couples produces an empty wallet.

There are some people who, for the most part, are travel companions only. I know of two women who never see each other except at Christmastime, when they always take a trip to Mexico or Spain. They are highly compatible in this area. This is rare, but it is a wonderful and special kind of friendship. These two women work hard to protect it.

CHAPTER 11

The Care and Maintenance of Your Friends

Most of us go through a large part of our lives wondering things like, *Does she like me? Why aren't people calling me? Is he being a good friend to me?* Or even, *How can I get more friends?*

It's really very simple. A friend is not something you acquire. A friend is who you *are*. To have friends, you must first *be* a friend.

This is such a basic human truth, yet it is one we all have such a hard time learning. Just in the way that love is not a noun but a verb, we must cultivate and care for friends if we want them to care for us.

Of course, if you are a very attractive, powerful, or rich person, you will always have people who will want to be around you who may *claim* you as a friend, but real friendship only comes when you are yourself being a real friend. Don't worry: Friendships don't take work as much as they take attention and caring; if it is a good friendship it doesn't feel like work but more like your favorite hobby.

How to Feed the Friendship

Think of your friendship as a delicate plant, a beloved pet, or even a small child—anything that can't survive unless it is taken care of. You can't just meet someone and expect the friendship to grow all on its own, any more than you can bring a flowering plant home from the store, plop it down in a dark corner, and expect it to thrive. You must take care of it if you want it to live. And, very much like a vegetable garden, if you feed your friendships, they will feed you.

Staying in Touch and Making Plans

As busy as you are with work, family, and everything else, you need to make sure you are tending your "friendship garden." In other words, you have to keep in touch with friends; don't always wait until they call you. Whatever system works for you, you must not let a good friend go by the wayside. You have to make sure you get to everyone, at least once in a while. Try to call or e-mail people you haven't talked to in a while. Most of the time it only takes a few minutes to e-mail or phone someone, just to say hello.

With very good friends, do be sure the other person is not always the person to initiate your playdates. There are many relationships in which a bad habit develops, and one person gets accustomed to the other calling to make plans. It may all seem to be working fine on the surface, but this is the kind of thing that can corrode a friendship.

When you do get busy and fail to keep in touch with a friend, and the friend calls or e-mails you, responding with either "We were just talking about you!" or "I was just thinking about you yesterday" will go a long way. If it feels as though a friend is trying to make you feel guilty because you haven't been in touch, remember that that person is just insecure—as many of us are much of the time. Reassurance, if you can muster it, can be more constructive than annoyance.

The Golden Rule: Reciprocity

If your friend is always inviting you to his house for dinner and you never invite him to yours, you may have a reciprocity problem. If someone is always insisting on picking up the check, you might want to try to grab the next one. There are, of course, some people you always have to call, who never call you, and yet when you spend time with them it is very nice. As long as you harbor no resentment this is fine, but these people will never be best friends. Reciprocity is necessary for a friendship to grow.

Being There for Your Friends

"Being there" does not have to mean helping your friend through major trauma. Little things mean a lot: calling a friend on her birthday, or calling a friend to find out how she is if she has been sick. When you check in with a friend to see how a big meeting went, or a special date, it makes him feel great. Compliment your friends whenever it's called for; don't assume that because you've know each other a long time they know you think they are wonderful.

Condolence notes are a must. If you ever have lost someone important in your life, you will know how important they are. Don't buy canned sentiments, even if you just write: "I am so sorry to hear the news. I am thinking about you." Many people get squirrelly around the subject of death and tell themselves it is better to do nothing, say nothing, rather than make a faux pas and say the wrong thing. Nothing could be further from the truth.

Forgiveness

If you have true intimacy in your friendships, you will probably sometimes feel hurt by a friend. Not only may you feel hurt, but you can feel so *right* in your sense of injustice. After all, how could your friend treat you so badly? How could she be so insensitive? Why didn't your friend call you when she knew you had hit a tough patch in your life? Is this her idea of friendship?

Part of being a friend is being able to forgive, especially the small transgressions. None of us is perfect; remember that you probably make friendship errors too—even if they may not be the same ones. It feels really good to let things go. Try to focus on all the things you value about your friendship with the person who has hurt you.

This does not mean it is acceptable for anyone to abuse you, take advantage of you, or mistreat you in any way. If the friend has transgressed, he will, it is hoped, say he is sorry. But if he doesn't you must try to forgive him. It is the loving thing to do. (Of course, so is saying you are sorry.)

Why Love Means Always Having to Say You're Sorry

SCENARIO 1

Adam walks into the restaurant, looking nervous. He is an hour late.

"Where in God's name have you been, Adam?" his friend Jill sputters. "I've been waiting for you for *two hours!*" (Note: Anger and frustration can lead people to exaggerate).

"Oh, sorry, I didn't realize I was so late," Adam says, trying to act casual. "But listen, I had this meeting with J.B. that went overtime, and then I couldn't get a cab for the life of me. Can I buy you lunch? Have you ordered?"

Jill stands up. "I've eaten," she says coldly. She puts her purse over her shoulder and walks toward the door. "And yes, you can buy."

SCENARIO 2

Adam runs into the restaurant, looking frantic. He is an hour late.

"Where in God's name have you been, Adam? I've been waiting for you for two hours!" Jill sputters.

"Jill! Oh, my God—I am so sorry! You must be starving... My cell phone is dead, so I couldn't call you, but I should have left the office much sooner than I did to get here. Can you forgive me? Do you still have time to hang out? Can I buy lunch?"

"That's okay," Jill says. "These things happen. I've had a sandwich but I'll get some coffee. I can stay a little longer, I guess."

"That's great!" says Adam, "I thought maybe I was so late I wouldn't get to see you. Thanks so much for understanding. I hated thinking of you waiting here for me."

When you accidentally step on someone's foot you say you're sorry. Likewise, when you step on someone's feelings, you should say you're sorry. The problem is that most of us are afraid of being weak, and we think if we admit we are wrong that we will lose ground. When your actions have caused someone stress or pain, accept culpability, then move on. We are all fallible. And don't just say the words, but mean them. Your friends can tell the difference.

If you are convinced you did nothing wrong, but your friend seems to need an apology nonetheless, here's a shocking idea: Go ahead and apologize anyway. Maybe you are in the wrong and you just can't see it. In any case, "I'm sorry" doesn't mean "I'm a bad person." To a friend, "I'm sorry" usually means "I love you."

The Truth Tightrope: Walking the Line Between Compassion and Honesty

Trying to decide whether to tell a good friend the truth about something can be incredibly hard. You have to weigh the benefits the friend may get from hearing the truth against the pain you may be causing her by telling it—as well as against any possible fallout for you, for being the bearer of this truth. As a general friendship rule, if you think telling her the truth will help her, then you must try to tell her, no matter how difficult. Otherwise, you should keep your trap shut.

For example, let's say your friend has recently married someone who is sarcastic and boorish to her and to everyone else. Your friend can't seem to see that fewer invitations are coming her way because of her unappetizing husband. Do you tell her? No, you do not. She is not about to divorce her husband (more's the pity); she loves him and therefore this "truth" will only serve to embarrass and possibly depress her—and will hurt your friendship.

On the other hand, perhaps you have another friend who has decided that her mission in life is to teach everyone she knows how to play the harmonica. She has taken to bringing harmonicas with her to dinner parties and forcing people to practice after coffee is served. As a result, you notice that she has not been invited to several dinner parties she would ordinarily have been invited to.

Do you tell her? Absolutely, but in private. "Sweetie, everyone loves you, but they hate this harmonica kick you are on. It's making you a pariah," should do it.

Singles and Couples:
How the World Should Be But Isn't

I have only anecdotal evidence to support this theory, but I think Americans are very unsophisticated when it comes to issues of socializing between couples and singles. Couples don't think: *Who should we see this weekend?* They think: *Which couples can we see this weekend?* It's the truth; couples love their single friends during the week, but on the weekends, when there is more time to relax and really enjoy a long dinner, couples like to see other couples. Europeans don't seem to do this as much. In fact, the most famous hosts will tell you that a mix of singles and couples is better than all of one or the other at a dinner party. And yet the last time I went to a large dinner at least three people expressed shock and displeasure at being separated from their spouses, as if they didn't already see enough of them the other 364 days of the year.

Does this sound like sour grapes? It is, but only partially: It's not only singles who are missing out on truly interesting evenings. Differences in lifestyle (not temperament) can really spruce up conversations. One remedy for this inequality is for single people to host more, inviting their couple friends over. It's best to invite two couples (remember what I said about triangles). If you have an extra single friend, throw him into the mix—not to make it even, but to extend a weekend night invitation to a fellow singleton.

Favors and Friends

When someone asks me to do something for him, my first impulse is to say yes. Like most people, I want to please. I like helping out my friends. And so, most of the time I do say yes. However, because I am not Gandhi, there is also, in my deepest core, a small part of me that expects the beneficiary of this favor to be there for *me* the next time *I* need a favor. This is not a good basis for doing something and will come back to bite me later. Unless it is a business transaction, generosity should come from love. Many people, when they do favors, see it in their minds as favors accruing, and they imagine the return will be waiting for them when they need it back. Psychologists call this "the favor bank" (though I think Tom Wolfe coined the term first). Beware the favor bank; you could lose your shirt!

There is, of course, a slight possibility—if you are someone in a position of influence or power—that people may want to be your friend because you can help them. Be wary of people who come into your life with whom you don't seem to have a real connection but who are all over you. If you suspect this, say no to any favors they ask of you until you get to know them better.

Try to follow these rules: Never do a favor for someone if you expect something in return other than, perhaps, a little gratitude. Never do a favor if you are going to resent doing it later; it must be free and clear.

Platonic Matchmaking: The Perils and Payoffs of Introducing Your Friends to Each Other

In a perfect world, everyone would meet everyone else's friends, and our social universes would expand exponentially. Unfortunately, that is not how it is—at least not in the part of the world I know. Most people have great reluctance, or at least substantial lethargy, about introducing their friends to each other.

The reluctance to "cross-pollinate" operates on several levels. For one thing, most people like to compartmentalize different areas of their lives to some degree. You may show different parts of yourself to different groups of friends. (I call this the Chameleon Complex, because if you are this type of person you will change in order to blend into different environments. When you are with many friends at once, you don't know what "color" to be.) You might have a vague idea that if your friends all got together you would be too exposed. And remember, since most people suffer from the Imposter Syndrome, many people may be afraid some of their friends will judge them for having other kinds of friends.

Then there is the impulse many people have about protecting territory. For example, if you have wonderful old friends who cook you squab every other Saturday and you treasure those evenings, it is natural human self-preservation not to want to share them. What if the people who you introduce to these old friends start horning in on your squab evenings? (After all, it's a pretty small bird.)

I love introducing my friends to each other, and I recommend it to everyone. But when you decide to do this, you do run the risk that the people you introduce to each other may become fast friends. And if (and this is key) they are not sharing *their* friends with *you*, you could end up feeling as if you got the short end of the stick.

Obviously all these blocks to opening up your social life are based on fear and should be dispelled, chased away, healed. Connecting your friends with each other is a nice thing to do for them and ultimately for yourself. So let's deal with some of the fears that may be keeping you from mixing your friends.

How to Survive Worlds Colliding
Is My Vault Safe?

One of the main concerns people have about socializing is the fear that private information one friend knows will be shared with others. This is not a wholly unjustified concern (especially if you are keeping a lot of secrets), but be assured that most of your friends will respect your privacy—the same way they want you to respect theirs. If you feel one of your friends is not a naturally discreet person, don't leave anything to chance. Instruct her specifically. Say "Look, you are meeting my friend tonight, but do not tell him anything about X, Y, and Z." Unless she is an idiot or a drunk, she should certainly be able to refrain from mentioning X, Y, and Z. And what's the worst that can happen? In most cases, if they are your friends they won't use anything they find out against you.

Don't Ask, Don't Tell

If Vera meets Jane and they become friends, will you feel left out when Vera and Jane start seeing each other one-on-one? If you are very confident, no. But sometimes the only way to make the whole "worlds colliding" thing work is for everyone involved to have a sort of unspoken "don't ask, don't tell" policy. When you are talking to Vera or Jane, they should not offer up the information that they are meeting for lunch the next day, unless you ask them. But neither should you ask them. It's not as if Vera and Jane are going behind your back. You know they have become friends, and you are happy they have become friends (or, at least, you're supposed to be happy about it). You know they are having a good time when they get together, just as you have a good time with each of them—or both of them, when you all three get together. You just don't need to know about their every meeting. The don't ask, don't tell policy staves off possible jealousy.

One Big, Happy Family

Introducing your friends to each other is one of those cooperative areas of life, like carpooling or potluck dinners. It only works if everyone is involved. However, when it does work, everyone benefits. Your friendships grow and become more permanent. If all your friends know each other, the circle of friends is cemented. You will have more parties to go to, and when the walls of compartmentalizing are torn down, the level of intimacy goes up. If you have known a friend for five years but have never met any of her other friends, you may not know all the facets of her. But when you meet her sister, her friends from college, and her friends from work, through them you will get to know her in a new way. The chances are good that you will love her friends because you love her, and they will love you because they love her.

So throw caution to the wind, put your friends in a room together, and feel the love!

CHAPTER 12

Embracing the Ebb and Flow of Friendship

One of the greatest joys in life is in making new friends. Every time we experience the growth of what we feel will be a sustaining friendship it is like a renewal of our deepest selves. However, one of the most difficult challenges in life is the loss of friends. We lose friends for different reasons: Sometimes they move far away (or we do) and we lose touch; sometimes the relationship just fades or ends abruptly.

I have found it helpful to think of life as a wide river. We are each in our own canoe going down the river. Sometimes we are going with the flow, other times we are fighting upstream, and still others it can feel as if we are pulling over for a rest. Other people—friends, family, lovers—flow beside us. They might flow beside us for just a while, or they might stay near us forever; but often the current takes them down the river at another speed, or down another fork, so that we drift apart. The wonderful thing is that there are other people we haven't met yet who are—or will soon be—coming near our canoes. And you never know; the ones who drifted away may come back, or we may catch up to them later.

The point is that sometimes your best friend gets married and has kids (and you don't), and suddenly you find your lifestyles are so different that even though you still love each other, your friendship fades. One friend moves to Paris, another friend pops up in your life after your not seeing him for twenty years. A relatively new friend becomes suddenly important to you for some reason (you share a lot, you validate each other, you learn from each other), while another friendship ebbs away. With the flow of life comes the flow of friends.

You will also have periods in your life that are more social than others. Sometimes you don't even know why it is that during one six-month period the phone hardly rings, but during the next you are busy with friends every other night. The real secret to happiness (which I for one am still trying to learn) is in leaning away: in allowing people to go on down the river when they want to go, and in opening yourself up to new people. We must recognize that change applies to friendships as well as to everything else in life.

Why All Friends Are Not Created Equal

One of the areas that gives us trouble is our expectations when it comes to the people in our lives. Often we are disappointed by a friend who we feel has not behaved the way we believe a friend should, and that disappointment hinders our continuing a relationship with him.

What is very helpful is to realize that you cannot expect all friends to be the same. Some friends will give more to you than you feel you are giving to them; some friends you will give more to them. Some people are better listeners than others; some are more entertaining. Some friends can offer sympathy; others can only provide practical help. Some friends can help you solve a problem; others are wonderful at showing appreciation when you help them. Some will take you to the hospital if you break your leg; some you could never expect to take care of you if you are sick. Some friends you will have to call all the time—they hardly ever call you; others will call you every week like clockwork. Some friends will make dates with you on a regular basis; others are passive—or elusive—and will happily respond but will never initiate. Some friends will make plans in advance; others will only see you on the spur of moment.

The hardest and most important lesson of friendship is not to keep score. You can't compare one friendship with another. Neither should you compare the qualities of your friend to your own friendship qualities. Never expect friends to get an "A" in every friendship subject. There is only one question to ask yourself regarding a friend: Do you enjoy this person, and do the joys of this person outweigh any negative factors?

Addressing Imbalances

On the other hand, if you are having a serious issue with a friend and you think it is something of which he is not aware, you should probably try to talk to him about it. A man I interviewed told me that after being frustrated with a good friend for years, for always reacting with aloofness to the problems he was having with his family, he confronted the friend about it. They worked it out and are better friends for having had the discussion. But it is never an easy thing to do. You have to have a good relationship base, something that makes it worth slogging through the uncomfortable moment. You also have to be careful to express yourself clearly, and not let anger carry you away. Usually you come out stronger, either because the issue gets better or because the person doing the confronting realizes that this is not something the person he is confronting can change.

Note: When a friend is not giving you what you feel you need, always try to remember what he has meant to you in the past. If he is suddenly grumpy all the time because of chronic back pain but he has really been there for you for fifteen years, you must think of it as if it were a marriage; to a certain extent, you have committed to this friend for better or worse.

Sometimes, rather than address imbalances, you may just have to try to press the "restart" button, if things are out of whack and you don't know why. One friend recently said to me, "I'm so mad at all my friends! None of them ever call me!" I told her there was only one thing to do: Call *them!*

Fair-Weather and Foul-Weather Friends

We all know about fair-weather friends. If everything is going well for you they are there, but as soon as life deals you a bad hand they are nowhere to be found.

But foul-weather friends can be just as frustrating in their own way as fair-weather friends. While fair-weather friends tend to disappear when you are in a bad mood, foul-weather friends have a "misery loves company" bent—and love nothing more than to commiserate about how hard life is. The trouble with foul-weather friends is that it usually only works well between you if you are both in a bad mood. And what fun, really, is that?

Your best friends should be able to relate to both your sunny and your rainy days—whether they are experiencing the same weather as you or not.

Dealing with Being Dumped by a Friend

Having to face that a good friend no longer wants to be friends can be as hard as losing a romantic partner—and sometimes harder.

Of course, often it is not so much a matter of being dumped but of the friend seeming to lose interest in the friendship. Sometimes you get the feeling that he is moving you down in priority in his life. When do you give up? When is it time to throw in the towel?

It is time to throw in the towel when you are certain that the friend has lost interest in the friendship, and it is not that he is merely perturbed at you for some reason. It takes two to tango, and if one person doesn't really want to dance it will not work. Making new friends can help take the sting away. But even if the relationship hadn't been working for you (so it isn't as if you are suddenly missing a whole lot of fun), you can still feel sad and bitter when you get the brush-off.

Try to figure out what happened. If you still value what you had, try to rectify the situation. Apologize if you can. Remember: Love has no pride; don't let it get in your way. However, there is also no use beating your head against the wall. Don't obsess. Sometimes the person pulling away is just doing what she has to do. It may have absolutely nothing to do with you, so try not to take it personally. She is simply flowing down the river at a different speed. Stay focused on what's happening with your own canoe.

Phasing Out People Who Are Not Enhancing Your Life

We change, friends change. The truth is that sometimes your friendship is no longer a good fit. One person gets more negative, another more positive. Your goals and values may be different than what they used to be. It could be a very old friendship that is no longer working. Or it could be someone you haven't known very long who you thought was going to be a good friend, but after some months of getting to know him better you realize it's just not enjoyable for you.

You can't be best friends with everyone. I come from a family of collectors: My father collects Victrolas, my sister collects antique dolls, my brother collects HO-gauge slot cars, my mother collects green glass. Me? I guess I collect people. When I find friends, I usually want to hoard them. I feel you can never have too many and that each one (no matter how quirky) is a treasure. But the fact of the matter is that a large collection of friends is hard to maintain. When a bedroom closet gets too full, you have to clean it out to make way for new things. All kinds of clutter are like this. Things must always be changing; No one starts and ends their life with the same ten friends. You outgrow people or they outgrow you.

Easing someone out of your life is difficult, if you are to achieve it with as little pain to the other person as possible. If you accept the premise of change, you can relish and love the friendship as it was, as it has been, while starting to spend less time with that person. You don't need to "break up"; you can just try less hard. Often things will fade in a natural, Darwin-like way.

Otherwise you may have to employ one of the following ending techniques.

The Platonic Breakup

For people who prefer things out in the open and like a clean break (even if it hurts a little more), this is like ripping the Band-Aid off fast. You just take a deep breath, sit the person down or call her on the phone (no e-mails for breakups, please), and explain as kindly as you can that you don't feel you have much in common anymore, that you are in different places, or whatever version of "it's not you, it's me" you care to use. Be kind. Don't break up with someone by telling them what a bad friend they are. You will be adding insult to injury.

The Slow-Down

No one likes to admit it, but most of us are familiar with this tapering-off technique. The slow-down is a standard—and the most gentle—method of dealing with unsatisfactory relationships. Here is an example of how this slow-motion fade-out is accomplished.

Let's say you and your life partner have, over the years, realized that you really have little in common with your friends Matt and Marcia. You have gone in one direction and they have gone in another, and you are often left with negative feelings when you spend time with them. You are ready to let them go from your life.

Since, naturally, you don't want to hurt Matt and Marcia's feelings, you gradually begin to scale back on the time you see them. What used to be a once-a-week get together becomes once every two weeks, then once a month. When they call, you are always very nice, but usually very busy. When they ask you to come to dinner, you schedule it as far in the future as possible, saying you are booked. For several months you may still spend a lot of time talking to Marcia or Matt on the phone, but less and less time seeing them in person. To keep your slow-down from being too noticeable, or hurtful, occasionally you initiate a call to one of them to ask how they are. On the other hand, you will often wait until Marcia calls two or three times before returning the call—always with apologies for being swamped with work, grandchildren, and other obligations. Your attitude toward Matt and Marcia remains very warm and loving, but eventually they become people you only see once or twice a year.

The slow-down can take months (sometimes years) to complete. Like bringing a deep-sea diver gradually up to the surface, you have to recede in very small increments to make this technique virtually pain-free. Obviously, how much time and effort you put into the slow-down will be in direct proportion to how deeply involved you were with the person to begin with. (If it's a family member, you could be slowing down for a decade.)

The Dance of Deferment

This technique consists of continually putting off a friend who wants to see you more than you want to see him. ("I know we said we were going to have lunch this week, but I'm totally crazed. Next week for sure.") If you are well practiced at the dance, you are probably using a lot of phrases like "I'll get back to you," "Maybe I'll see you this weekend," "We'll have to grab a cup of coffee next week," "We'll talk soon, I promise," and even the hackneyed, "Let's have lunch sometime."

This can get exhausting if it goes on too long. If the object of your dance does not seem to want to let go of your canoe, you may have to use the Platonic Breakup (page 245).

When Your Friends Couple Up (or Break Up)

When people go through major relationship changes, it affects all their friendships. If the beloved couple who everyone thought would be together forever breaks up, it can cause social tidal waves for the couple's friends. How do you make sure you don't lose a valued friend in a divorce? And, conversely, when your dearest friend in the world suddenly becomes part of a couple, is your friendship going to be changed forever? What if the new spouse doesn't like you?

Part of embracing the ebb and flow of life is being able to adjust to the inevitable changes in some of your friends' marital/relationship status. Sometimes it means the friendship will grow and strengthen in a new way; other times it means the friendship will dwindle.

Staying Friends with Both Exes

Like rubbing your stomach with one hand while tapping yourself on the head with the other, staying friends with both parties in a divorce or break-up takes an effort of concentration, coordination, and motivation most people don't have. It's a delicate situation, whether the break-up has been an acrimonious take-no-prisoners affair or a highly civilized mutual dissolution.

It's important to maintain good boundaries. Perhaps one weekend you see the ex-husband with friends in Assateague; the next weekend you have the ex-wife to your townhouse in Georgetown. While you do need to let them know you are continuing a relationship with each of them, you must avoid talking about one of them to the other—a very hard thing to do since your lives have been so intertwined for so many years. You may have a slightly guilty feeling as you juggle both friends, as if you are somehow having your cake and eating it too—almost as if you are having an affair.

More often what happens is that you like one person from the couple better than the other (you may actually have been secretly hoping for a break-up), and the decision about which person to go with is an easy one. However, it is still unsettling to have a now single friend when you are used to that person being part of a couple. It may bring up insecurities about your own relationship status, and it may just simply be less fun for you to have this couple become a single. Any time there is a shift in a friend's romantic relationship, it changes the structure of your social life. Your friend who was available only once a month may now want to spend every weekend with you. Or the formerly cheerful, carefree girl you knew is suddenly sullen and bitter. When the foundation of a friendship gets shaken, it takes effort to repair the cracks.

On rare occasions, your choice of which person in the ex-couple to remain friends with can be murky. One may be your friend from elementary school, but if you feel more affinity and affection for the other one, don't let longevity supercede preference. Above all, try to embrace the new configuration.

Being the New Guy

You've fallen in love at last; she is "the one." Unfortunately, all her closest friends are used to her being with someone else—namely, her very charming ex. How do you try to fit in? How can you compete with this precursor, who has such a strong bond with your true love's friends?

The answer is, you can't. Don't even try. If your mate's friends are real friends, they will not make you feel as if you are stepping into anyone else's shoes. Don't try to be anyone other than who you are. This can be one of the most challenging tests of a new relationship: trying to become assimilated into your new mate's pre-existing social life. Almost always, what happens is that the change causes some kind of shift—slight or not so slight—in the new couple's group of friends. Some will fall away, while others will survive.

No Longer an Extra

Your relationship with your long-term friends can change when you suddenly have a partner. The friend who expects you to always be available as a backup when her spouse had an emergency meeting is put out that you now have plans of your own. Entering a relationship means a new dynamic with your friends, and you should be aware that some people may have odd reactions. They may be happy for you but at the same time resent the fact that you no longer have as much time to focus on their needs and problems.

When Your Husband Hates Her Husband

It's a very common problem: you are best friends with someone but your spouses don't have anything in common—or they might actively dislike each other. This makes socializing in couple formations less than fun for all of you. Most of the time, the best course of action is for the best friends to see each other one-on-one whenever possible. In addition, the friends can try to organize group events that involve other couples, thereby keeping the foursome evenings to a minimum. And if the spouses are good sports, they will do their best for the sake of the happiness of their loved ones.

Social-Life Self Exam: Identifying Your Friendship Patterns—and Breaking Out of Them

It's true that change is the main element of life, but that doesn't mean it's not the thing we resist the most. Even when it comes to your social life, you need to make sure you are not stuck in a rut— or, to use the river metaphor, an eddy. Sometimes if you start to do things a little differently it can open up your life like magic.

Do you tend to socialize always in the same way—as far as where you go and what you do? Try doing something different the next time you meet a new friend. If you never think of going to a museum, go to a museum. If you have never been bowling, why not suggest it? Do you always have coffee on the first playdate, then lunch, then a movie? Just for the heck of it, go down a different path. Do new things. Go for a walk in the park, or go to a lecture.

Similarly, what are your friendship patterns? Do you find that when you get excited about a new friend, you call and e-mail them incessantly for a week and then let the whole thing drop? If so, the next time you meet a new person, proceed more slowly. If you are someone who has trepidations about her friends meeting each other, when you make a new friend, throw him together with your old friends right away. See what happens. If you begin to change small things, big changes can sometimes occur.

How to Create Friendship Flow Energy

So there you are, floating down the river of life in your canoe. What can you do, if anything, to cause friends to flow toward you more than they flow away from you?

There is a mountain of books as tall as Everest that will all tell you in great detail about having self-love and being loving to attract people. But let me put it this way: *You have to make your canoeing look good.* People trying to navigate in their own canoes aren't going to want to get too close to you if you are flailing around, causing dangerous waves and splashes, and yelling, "Help me, I don't know how to steer this thing!"

If you are positive and *interested* in people, they will be attracted to and interested in you. If you are happy, that is a powerful allure; people will be attracted. But here's a secret: You can fake a positive attitude for a while if you have to. When you pretend to be happy, you sometimes can attract enough people to you that you will actually get happier! (Although you can't fake it forever.)

To create friendship flow, you also must be sure you are letting go of things or people who are not contributing to your happiness. It is an amazing thing how the Universe works, but as soon as you let go of relationships that are not working, new people show up almost immediately. You have made room for them to flow into your life.

Playmates for Life

There are some people who, as soon as you meet them, you know are going to be your best friends. Whether it's past lives, chemistry, or just a juncture of timing, commonality, and sensibility that serve to make two people recognize each other as deeply harmonious spirits, these meetings are the great blessings of life. Yet even these perfect matches need care and feeding. Never forget that good friendships are sacred. They are more important than anything. Everything else—your job, money, accomplishments, entertainment, travel, knowledge—is the body of your life, but friends are its blood.

Not everyone is a friend at first sight; it may take ten or twenty years to know that this is someone who is going to be your playmate for life. But even when you do meet someone with whom you immediately feel you are going to be friends forever, circumstances may intercede. My oldest and dearest friend from childhood moved to California and then went through a series of life changes that were so different from my own experience—changes that also made her want to separate from her past—that I lost her, more or less. However, she is still what I consider a playmate for life, my friend Margo, because I know absolutely, without one speck of doubt, that if we were in a situation where we could spend a day together, we would both start giggling and crying until our stomachs hurt, and I would feel that indescribable and life-affirming bond of intimacy that makes our social selves go round. When I am old and gray, the only "social security" I need for certain is the security of my wonderful fellow hosts and guests, of my best friends—my playmates for life.

Most thinking people are continuously searching for meaning, wondering what will be left of them when they are gone, wondering if they will they make a mark on the world. Know this: The life you build with the people you love is your most important life project—one that sustains you, feeds you. Authentic connection with people is what matters. You can't count on wealth or health; you can count on friendship, whether the friends are your family or not. The relationships you build in your life are, in the end, the only things that matter.

Life *is* friends.